FROM SHRUG TO THE MOON

THE ROBERT NICHOLS STORY

FROM SHRUG TO THE MOON

THE ROBERT NICHOLS STORY

STEVE SPITHRAY

Published in paperback in 2021 by Sixth Element Publishing.

Sixth Element Publishing
Arthur Robinson House
13-14 The Green
Billingham TS23 1EU
www.6epublishing.net

© Steve Spithray 2021

ISBN 978-1-914170-20-1

British Library Cataloguing in Publication Data. A catalogue record for this book is available from the British Library.

All rights reserved. No part of this publication may be reproduced, stored in a retrieval system or transmitted, in any form or by any means, electronic, mechanical, photocopying, recording and/or otherwise without the prior written permission of the publishers. This book may not be lent, resold, hired out or disposed of by way of trade in any form, binding or cover other than that in which it is published without the prior written consent of the publishers.

Steve Spithray asserts the moral right to be identified as the author of this work.

Printed in Great Britain.

FOREWORD

My introduction to the world of Rob Nichols came via reading the *Fly Me To The Moon* fanzine, and also his weekly *On The Beat* dispatches in my nana's copy of the *Evening Gazette*. She would save the weekend culture guide for me, knowing my love of music. There's a lot of affection for Rob. Anyone who devotes themselves to a labour of love like *Fly Me To The Moon* will be appreciated, even if only by a cult audience. Once, I was at a charity event with Rob, and a smiling Tony Mowbray came up to us and had a little chat with him – how many other former managers are on friendly terms with fanzine editors, I wonder?

Added to that, his support of the Teesside music scene has made him even more recognisable and respected. He's always been very positive about my different musical projects when I've bumped into him, which means a lot. After moving up to Newcastle for university, I've always been interested in what's happening back home, so being able to connect with the football and music through his writing and personality is important to me. He's a subcultural force of nature!

Paul Smith, Maximo Park

AUTHOR'S NOTE

As a new decade dawned, the giant blue dragonfly sat quietly rusting, swaying gently in the wind as its foundations slowly dissolved in the estuary sands. Half-a-mile along the river the graffitied metal skeletons at the dinosaur park mirrored the industrial remains that littered the abandoned old town, the moth-eaten ship, the crumbling Vulcan Street wall and what remained of Bolckow & Vaughan's original blastworks. Open ruins. The ghosts of yesteryear hiding in plain sight.

At Acklam Cemetery, within cheering distance of Middlesbrough FC's old Ayresome Park ground, mourners gathered. Apart from it being freezing cold and the rain coming sideways in sheets, the windswept end plot far away from the cover of the trees was an inauspicious end for another eighty-odd years of history. A mound of earth lay indiscreetly covered by an old weather-worn tarpaulin where more mourners should have been and two burly men placed the coffin on two wooden stands… the type decorators use. The vicar braced against the bitter wind, "Ashes to ashes, dust to dust…" And as the flowers landed with dull thuds on the coffin lid, a digger engine fired up a little too close for comfort. A working-class dystopia that should all be in black and white for posterity. The circle of life in a northern working-class town.

Fast forward a couple of months and Robert and I

parted company for what would be the last time for a number of long months. We briefly referenced a virus of some such but were more occupied with the mayor of Middlesbrough's alleged involvement in a business on the corner at the traffic lights where my car was parked one way and his the other. Then we lightly pencilled in another date, as had become our custom.

We had been meeting haphazardly once a month or so at Bedford Street Coffee on a Sunday morning for brunch, although we never ate. We shared hot chocolates. By 'shared', I mean we had one each, then a second and sometimes a third. We swapped titbits of our lives as I tried to incorporate a structured conversation into our rendezvous and keep Robert on topic as his mind continued to sift out reams of seemingly unrelated stories of intrigue, bluster and happenchance that would be difficult for many to believe but, to Robert, were just another day at work, as it quickly became apparent that the music part of his life could probably warrant a book of its own. As a rule, our conversations would be interrupted at least once by a stranger approaching to talk about football. Robert was forever amiable and apparently constantly prepared for such interruptions, as I wondered if the other party ever realised they were being recorded. And Robert always had time for a quick chat… his memory throughout was impeccable as I mentally calculated how many people he must meet and how he remembered everybody's name and the conversations they had. After our sessions, Robert would always depart to see his elderly dad with the same quiet sadness, and I would wonder what might happen to Robert's story, as he too gets older, if it were not written down now.

"I have a recurring nightmare of forgetting about a match and almost missing the kick off," he says. "It would be the most horrific thing imaginable to me. Having come close to missing games since my last in 1999, I have felt so panicky but Covid-19 puts it all into perspective. I would ordinarily have felt absolutely devastated but people's lives are more important."

Luckily, we had done most of our required face-to-face meetings so we kept in touch during lockdown through a series of Q&A style interviews so that the end of this part of my journey through Robert's life signalled the start of this book, as we conversed during and post-lockdown to tie up a few loose ends. The disruption to the football season and live music meant my writing schedule was completely up in the air, as was Robert's financial security… his main income coming from his Middlesbrough FC fanzine, Fly Me To The Moon. I wasn't even sure if this book was still viable without the guaranteed football fans and gig audiences as potential readers…

ACKNOWLEDGEMENTS

Claire Dupree-Jeans (NARC. Magazine), Gordon Dalton at Creative Factory, Oli Heffernan, Chris Bartley, Gary Miller (Whisky Priests), Michael Sanderson, Richard Pink, Kev Wall, Ajay Saggar, Bob Fischer, Lindsey Dixon, Paul Smith (Maximo Park), Geoff Vickers, Vladimir Janak (Boro Miro), Joe Bell, Yvonne Ferguson (MFC), Alan Fearnley, Bjarte Hjartoy, Elaine Palmer, Paul Armstrong, ROJOR, Michael at Overground Underground, Craig Hornby, Kingsley Chapman, Mark Underwood, Harry Pearson, Martyn Hudson Watts, Michael Baines, Tracy Hyman, Rosanne Lightfoot (Swift Tees), Matthew Smith, Steve Sherlock, Sharon Caddell, Neil Spithray, Vivienne Hardman, Louise Wilkin, Nigel Downing… and Emma Dolby for putting up with all of this!

CONTENTS

Prologue: Eindhoven, 2006 1

1. Marton-In-Cleveland, 1962 3
2. Newcastle, 1977 11
3. Linthorpe Village, 1986.. 20
4. East Berlin, 1989... 31
5. Sea of Tranquillity, 1987 52
6. York, 1985... 59
7. Reading, 1999 78
8. Newport, 1994 85
9. Middlehaven, 1995.. 115
10. Cardiff, 2004 125
11. Stromness, 2018 144
12. Middlesbrough, 2015... 153
13. Toft House, 2020... 165
14. Linthorpe Village, 2021 178
15. Middlesbrough, Present Day.................................... 186
Epilogue... 189
Shrug Discography 191

PROLOGUE: EINDHOVEN, 2006

"That is it… it's Eindhoven. It's Eindhoven. Boro have made it. One of the most glorious nights in the history of football. We go back to 1876, the Infant Hercules, fathomed out of the foundries of Teesside, mined out of the Eston Hills, we're roaring all the way to Eindhoven and the UEFA Cup Final. It's party, party, party! Everybody round my house for a parmo!"

It seems strange to start a biography with the words of someone else but when Middlesbrough Football Club qualified for the final of the UEFA Cup in April 2006, it was Teesside broadcasting legend Ali Brownlee's immortal commentary that cemented the night in local history. And it was the match, Rob Nichols would tell me some years later, that is his greatest football memory of them all.

Just twelve days later, the streets around the Philips Stadion in Eindhoven's Frederiklaan district were awash with red and white as Rob squared what had essentially been a twenty-year circle. From the dusty terraced streets surrounding the club's old Ayresome Park ground in Linthorpe – where the gates had been padlocked by the administrators in 1986 – to the opening of the new flagship Riverside Stadium in the wastelands of Middlehaven in 1995, a League Cup win in 2004 and to the UEFA Cup Final itself. Throughout the land, supporters of clubs like

Middlesbrough understand that it's not the winning of the big cups that matters, so much as the small victories along the way. So, a semi-final win or the big scalp becomes the residual memory as much as the final itself. The final, of course, was something of an anti-climax and the club have since struggled to reach the same heights but, for thousands of other Middlesbrough fans like Rob, it was another day in a lifetime's commitment.

The following week, three hundred and fifty miles away back in Middlesbrough, Rob would be part of a small group assembled for the unveiling of Gareth Southgate as the club's new manager… a man who divides the fans as much today as he did at the time. Robert's fanzine, Fly Me To The Moon, had already been his main source of income for many years, so, with no regular day job to return to, Rob spent the summer conjuring ideas for his band, Shrug. And perhaps a trip to Hong Kong to visit his brother.

And that is essentially the diamond and the arc of this story… the dual loves of football and music jockeying for dominance like a binary star system. As we will see, it is often football that just about comes out on top. This book is about Robert (as is his wont, although virtually everybody else I spoke to referred to him as Rob) but it is also intrinsically and essentially about Teesside and its people…

1. MARTON-IN-CLEVELAND, 1962

The sunlight skitters off the new country club in leafy Marton Village a few yards from where Captain James Cook was born over two hundred years before. Fields stretch off to the south towards Nunthorpe, and Roseberry Topping is visible to the east. It's July 1962, the middle of a largely uneventful summer, and, in nearby Chestnut Drive, Robert Andrew Nichols is coming kicking and screaming onto this mortal coil.

Just north of Thirsk on the A19, you start seeing the word Teesside on road signs, not Middlesbrough or Stockton or the myriad satellite market towns and villages that surround the twin towns. Just Teesside. The pulsing nervous system that connects Darlington and Yarm, and Hartlepool and Redcar. Teesside. Further north it splits and you can head for either the Municipal Buildings in Stockton or the Town Hall in Middlesbrough. The Boro… where our story begins. Only in 1830 was the first house built in West Street, spitting distance from where the iconic Transporter Bridge would later stand and near where Middlesbrough FC's Riverside Stadium sits now. However, by the time William Gladstone visited in 1862 (almost exactly one hundred years before Rob arrived) and uttered those famous words that would come to define the town, "This remarkable place, the youngest child of England's enterprise, is an infant but if an infant, an infant Hercules," the town was thriving as the blast furnaces raged all the way from Teesport to St Hilda's, turning ore from Cleveland's hills into iron and steel to be shipped around the world.

By the early 1960s, Middlesbrough would have been a doggedly engaging but rough-cut of a town. The first wave of Victorian prosperity had subsided and a staunchly working-class veneer applied. England were yet to win the World Cup, The Beatles were just starting along their road to world domination and Robert's soon to be beloved Middlesbrough FC were languishing mid-table in the old Division 2 of the Football League. The town's biggest employer at the time was ICI, employing 29,000 people – nearly all men – while the industrial estuary stretched from the mouth of the river past Seal Sands through Wilton and Port Clarence, and by now the town's Dorman Long steelworks had already been used to build iconic buildings all over the world, from Sydney Harbour to bridges in Africa and a small railway station in Brazil. Chestnut Drive was part of new Middlesbrough, with the chocolate box village of Marton quickly becoming a dormitory suburb expanding rapidly from the 1950s onwards.

Janet Nichols was a doting mother to Robert (and brother Stephen, who was born two years later). Janet sadly passed away in April 2015 from cancer after a long illness but was, by all accounts, a formidable woman. Far from being a 1960's housewife, Janet was a fierce paternal counterpart, very organised and going on to become a partner in an employment agency, Link Technical Services. She had been brought up in Levick Crescent, Whinney Banks, and her mother and father used to look after Robert and Stephen there many weekends and, later when they moved to Redcar, the brothers would sometimes stay during school holidays.

Robert's dad, Neville Nichols (christened Alfred after his dad but using his middle name), had been in the RAF in National Service in the 1950s. He was a keen boxer. Some of Robert's earliest memories are of his dad going to watch Middlesbrough before coming back, seemingly every Saturday, uttering the old club motto, "Never again," before loyally returning the following week. By this time, Neville was a marketing manager for ICI Petrol – where else – and would fascinate a young Robert with photos of ICI and Imperial petrol tankers.

Neville had grown up in Brambles Farm in east Middlesbrough. His mother later moved to Beechwood but his aunts all lived there into their nineties. Robert's paternal grandfather, Alfred Sr, fought and was wounded several times in World War 1 (although he never talked about it) and later worked in the blast furnaces. He was one of the first car owners in the new Brambles Farm estate in the 1940s and he and Robert's paternal grandmother were already retired when Robert was born. Dad Neville still lived in Marton until recently, although he no longer attends the match.

"He's in his mid-80s, he's got a bit of dementia and he

can't drive anymore. It's sad," Rob tells me. "He'd gone for many, many years."

Everyone had moved in more or less together in Chestnut Drive and the surrounding streets – The Willows and Oak Avenue – and Rob remembers lots of friends of a similar age. Indeed, many of the parents had forged a community together at the weekly dances at Marton Hotel & Country Club and they all became very good friends, while many of the dads also worked for ICI. These were times of real community spirit and camaraderie.

"We had a field behind our gardens," Rob says, "where we could build dens, an orchard with trees, an old ruined farm and then a building site to explore. We would play on the field or in the road. Or kick balls against the wall, if there was no one else around. Someone would always be a commentator and cry out 'the keeper is equal to it', mimicking the football on TV as the keeper made a full length save. We would mostly just make a goal from a lamppost to a jumper and play three pots and you are in until it started to get dark and one by one our mams called us in for tea. There were a lot less cars, I suppose, but obviously we had lots of breaks in play for traffic."

Occasionally, the friends would all walk down to Stewart Park, which took about twenty minutes, and play big games of football.

It was a whimsical and carefree childhood as the country enjoyed the first real fruits of post-war prosperity, but a working-class upbringing nonetheless.

Robert and brother Stephen attended Captain Cook Infant School in Marton and then moved up to Captain Cook Junior School next door. Perhaps unsurprisingly, they were fed a constant stream of James Cook trivia that shaped an early interest in local history that has stayed with Robert until this day. Rob recalls, "In assemblies, the teachers would talk about the great explorers and I always remember Mr Oversby, the Head, comparing the size of the school to Cook's ship, The Endeavour. We also had a lump of rock from Point Hicks in Australia, the first point observed from The Endeavour in eastern Australia."

The boys then moved up to Nunthorpe Comprehensive School, and Robert was in the first comprehensive year after it converted from a secondary modern. This was not an easy transition as Rob remembers it. "The years above us were none too happy at being invaded by a comprehensive year. There were about a thousand of us in a school built for far less. So, until a couple of years later when a big new block was built, we were pretty much crammed together and the queues for lunch were lengthy."

It's worth noting that although Robert was attending Middlesbrough games by this time, it had not become the all-consuming passion it would be later... partly because he was, he says, "absolutely appalling" at playing the game itself.

"I might have kicked around a lot but we all did," he says. "I was usually last pick for any games, either at school or in the street."

On the music front, Robert's parents had a lot of

records at home. Records were still quite a costly hobby at the time. "Mainly my mam, I suppose… Jack Jones. Everyone's mam liked Jack Jones in those days." But he also remembers Bread, Carpenters, Frank Sinatra, Perry Como and Tony Bennett. A firm musical grounding. Then, at school, he would sing hymns in assembly or, as a treat, Yellow Submarine would sometimes be played when it was raining and he and his classmates had to sit cross-legged on the hard wooden hall floor instead of playing out. Radio was also an important part of the Nichols household.

"Mainly the Radio 2 breakfast show," Rob says, "where the music would be quite traditional, I suppose."

In 1973, in an epiphany of sorts, Robert recalls his dad taking him out to work with him. As a rep for ICI Petrol, Neville was responsible for signing up petrol stations and would drive round making sure they were all operating efficiently and profitably. Rob remembers his dad bringing work home to design garage livery for the pumps and even dabbling in signage.

"ICI was like that, you could have a broad remit. Anyway, we went to Sunderland and it was half-term holidays so, while he went in all the garages between South Hylton and Durham, I sat in the car and listened to daytime radio." Rob remembers this day so distinctly as the first time he heard bands that would go on to become early favourites of his – ELO (Showdown), Status Quo (Break The Rules) and Nazareth (the Joni Mitchell cover, This Flight Tonight).

After leaving Nunthorpe Comprehensive with the requisite collection of O-Levels, Robert then went on to sixth form at South Park in Normanby. He remembers, "It was a great big place in an inter-war building and, only having a couple of hundred students, it was so much better than school."

Perhaps feeling more at home in the less intense environment of a sixth form college, Rob felt confident enough to make his stage debut there in an end of year review. "I banged a drum and then came out from behind the kit to sing a Buzzcocks song, Times Up from the Spiral Scratch EP. I put on a tracksuit and recited John Cooper Clarke's I've Got A Brand New Tracksuit. Richard Pink and Robert March were also involved. Richard was playing guitar, and had been playing since he was about eleven, I think, so was pretty proficient. Robert also played guitar. They both had electric guitars and amps. I was so nervous. Just like before the first Shrug gig. Kind of praying it would somehow be cancelled. But it wasn't and it was a real buzz when we were not booed off but, in fact, earned kind applause."

Even if he didn't realise at the time, Richard Pink and Robert March would soon become an important part of the Robert Nichols story.

Around the same time, a member of the public had come onto campus, seemingly unchallenged, and started threatening some of the students.

"The guy didn't have a gun or a knife or anything," Rob remembers. "He must just have walked into the building.

There was a side door where you could walk in rather than go to reception… maybe not great, security wise. He wandered in and was menacing. People were afraid. But I just started talking to him about football and he talked back, shaking his head. He forgot about threatening everyone and soon walked away out of the building. I think he walked away before police responded to the staff call. I was so pissed off about [a recent] match that I talked to him about it. We had that in common so by then he was shaking his head rather than shaking his fists, I suppose."

Robert studied A-Levels in History, Geography and Art – his three favourite subjects – before embarking on pastures new, enrolling on a History and Geography Joint Honours degree at Leeds University. It was to be a real awakening for Robert, although he had to defer one year after getting food poisoning during his exams. He passed his Art A-Level with an E, "So that was good enough for a pass," but took ill right at the start of his History exam. While he valiantly tried to complete his other exams, he could hardly see the paper so his handwriting was unreadable. So, Robert retook History and Geography, supplemented by S-Level History and a French O-Level. "I was offered a course at Sheffield Poly, through clearing and an interview, but decided to wait a year and take the exams again," Rob explains. He also now recalls taking, and then stupidly dropping, Archaeology as a second subject in his first year… something else that would later become a passion.

2. NEWCASTLE, 1977

Something else that happened in Robert's later school years, and a logical next step after those school holidays going to work with his dad and travelling all over with the radio on and the windows down absorbing all the music he could, was the beginning of a lifelong love affair with live music that would see Rob not only perform and sing in his own band but become a mainstay in the local music scene… a go-to for advice, a motivator and a doyen of all that is Teesside music.

If 1976 had been a seminal year for music with the Sex Pistols rewriting the playbook for the youth, perhaps the biggest cultural shift since The Beatles thirteen years before, 1977 would see the second wave of punk, and the emergence of perhaps some of the most influential bands of that decade, such as The Clash, and a raft of more politically motivated and musically minded young talent.

While the newsreels and tabloid headlines portrayed something of an overnight cultural earthquake, the truth for Robert and many other music fans at the time was that it ushered in a more transitional period of culture and politics that would later reflect the eclecticism and performance of his own post-punk band when they started out eight years later. The truth is there wasn't just one day the world woke up and punk had arrived. By the early 1970s, John Peel was already championing anything and everything risqué or avant garde in the UK, and, as anyone who has listened to Nuggets, The Sonics, MC5 or early Stooges will tell you, in America, the punk ethos had been alive and well since the post-war days of Jack Kerouac and Neal Cassady.

In February 1977, Robert stepped through the grand pillared doors of Newcastle City Hall for the first time to see Rory Gallagher… his first gig. This was closely followed by Uriah Heep on March 9th of the same year at the same venue.

"The City Hall," he says, "was the main seated gig venue in the North East at that time. That was where all the big touring acts went."

Rory Gallagher, at this time was something of a live aficionado, while Uriah Heep were touring their Firefly album, which was ironically a throwback to the band's early 1970s sound. Rob can laugh now about a potential lack of taste in those days.

"Look, don't tell anyone this," he tells me as my Dictaphone whirs on the table in front of us and I have my publisher on speed-dial, "but after starting out with some good taste, my friends and me all went through a prog-rock downfall. It was the early 70s and the way things went was first you got into old Beatles albums, then there was a progression – or regression – to ELO, then into 'heavier' stuff like early Genesis, Deep Purple, Led Zeppelin and Black Sabbath. At the other end of my street in Marton, Mark Underwood lived on the corner of Oak Avenue – he was born two weeks after me – and his parents had an extension built onto their house, and, in there, was a music room with a big music centre. And that is where the two of us, and other mates like Ian Atkinson, would listen to our music through his dad's big speaker system."

Mark Underwood remembers, "I think the first time I became aware of pop music was hearing Blockbuster by Sweet and Rubber Bullets by 10CC which I recall listening to walking home from Captain Cook's school in Marton with Rob. Our musical tastes evolved as we got older and I can recall listening to my Beatles Red and Blue greatest hits albums whilst playing pool with Rob and Stephen, his younger brother, in the lounge at his parents' house on Chestnut Drive. Rob introduced me to bands he liked at the time, including ELO through their Face the Music album and Be Bop Deluxe through their Sunburst Finish album. I played him albums like The Lamb Lies Down On Broadway by Genesis, and Timeless Flight by Steve Harley. We were not into the coolest music at that time but another friend Martin Kellerman, who also lived on Chestnut Drive, did introduce us to David Bowie."

Of course, some of these bands – like Black Sabbath and Led Zeppelin – were keen to shock and subvert in the same way punk would later. Punk was a knee jerk reaction to the overblown procrastinations of the prog-rock that came before, which itself was merely the culmination of a protracted period of experimentation and determination to be wilder and further out there at all costs. Punk would go on to suffer the same fate as prog, as it gradually dissipated into a cartoon version of itself, followed by its own protracted period of metamorphosis (particularly with the emergence of the New Romantics in the early 1980s). Irrefutable proof, if it were needed, that all revolutions eat themselves.

However, it's this kind of serendipitous good fortune, in terms of access to lots of good music, that seems to be a common thread from a young age in all big music fans' lives, particularly musicians. Robert continues, "Mark preferred heavier guitar bands and we were getting into all this whilst listening to Brian Anderson's Tees Rock Show on BBC Radio Cleveland. We would tape the show and buy up loads of back catalogues through Frantic Music mail order. We would discuss each show, walking the two-and-a-half miles to school clutching an NME or Melody Maker (later Sounds, too). We would be joined by other friends along the route. This was all in 1976 and 1977 – when punk was emerging – though initially not on our radar at all. We were just getting into rock, and were tracking through back catalogues… and then punk burst through."

However, for Robert and his friends, it would not be until the more melodic Stranglers broke through later in 1977 – and helped popularise the poppier sentiments of the broader punk genre – that the tide really began to turn.

Rob says, "Richard Pink was too cool for this route. He had slicked back hair and a haversack with Patti Smith,

The Velvet Underground, Symbionese Liberation Army (SLA) written on it. He liked Bowie and Lou Reed. He talked about Iggy Pop. That was cool."

Although clearly still a time of some musical conflict, all of us will have gone one way or another as teenagers. Robert recalls voting in the NME and Melody Maker end-of-year polls at a time when the papers would pour scorn on the readers who voted for the likes of the Sex Pistols, The Stranglers and Genesis in the favourite bands category.

"We stayed quiet about this," Rob reflects, "but it was all due to the age we were at… we were getting into music in a big way in 1976, searching backwards and forwards. We would eventually throw our lot in with punk, but, by 1977 and 1978, it was post-punk, new wave and alternative that was emerging. That would be the music of choice from then on. After a summer of playing any great punk in 1977, it was anything post-punk and alternative we could get our hands on."

So, let's go backwards before we go forwards. Robert's first memories of music were at home while his dad was at work, but his first tentative steps into music collecting would be an altogether more personal experience.

"I remember going to Woolco in Thornaby, he says, "and that was like stepping into the future. A land of concrete, underground car parks ascending right into the shop itself, with absolutely everything under one flat roof. Even the name itself sounded like it was flash."

Thornaby is a new town that looks, to the outsider, like it may have sprung up overnight between the wars, but, in actual fact, it has a rich market and RAF history. Thornaby's Woolco was the company's second store.

"There was a little record section there," Rob remembers, "and, although it was likely to be my parents' money and not mine, I bought the Stealers Wheel LP, Ferguslie Park. I can remember being disappointed Stuck in the Middle wasn't on it, but I still loved it. Star was the main single from it. Back On My Feet Again and Blind Faith were tunes I really liked. This was Gerry Rafferty and Joe Egan. And on the cartoon cover, they were drawn with a giant cow. I also bought Status Quo's Hello. Both were in 1973 so I was ten going on eleven years old at the time. I played them both half to death."

Next up for Robert was Eric Clapton, supported by Ronnie Lane's Slim Chance in April of the same year. But this was not without its stresses.

"I had shingles before these ones," he says, "and it meant I had to declare myself fit for a school trip after only two days off."

In fact, these were Robert's first days off through illness in four years at school. He was evidently trying to equal his grandma's record of never taking a day off sick at school, and was also perhaps an early indicator of his other quest for records… such as not missing a single Middlesbrough FC match home and away between September 1999 until lockdown in March 2020. He made it on the trip in the end, remembering being taken in a minibus with all his friends, organised by the school art teacher, "and platform shoed, long haired guitar player Keith 'Geordie' Neasham, who was basically just taking us to see two of his guitar heroes."

Mark adds, "I can recall my first three gigs… and I suspect they were also Rob's first three gigs too. Rob took art at Nunthorpe Comprehensive and his art teacher was into music and got tickets for gigs at Newcastle City Hall for himself and some students. I think that as fourteen-year-olds, we would have been keen to go to see anyone play live but the gigs were Manfred Mann's Earth Band, supported by Racing Cars on 18th September 1976, Uriah Heep supported by Woody Woodmansey's U-Boat on 9th March 1977, and Eric Clapton, supported by Ronnie Lane's Slim Chance, on 24th April 1977. Clearly we were at the mercy of the art teacher's taste but arguably got lucky with the Clapton gig."

Rob says, "I loved Uriah Heep after that gig and bought a few albums. They had a great organ sound. I always loved Hammond and keyboards high in the mix."

But the first gig you could call a punk gig for Rob, as if by a fateful alignment of the post-punk planets, was not until his favourites The Stranglers came to Middlesbrough Town Hall in the summer of 1977, and as Rob chats keenly as if it was only yesterday, an understated enthusiasm permeates his speech that absorbs the listener.

"It was the tour for Rattus Norvegicus, the album that really turned our heads," he says. "Brian Anderson used to smash up Iggy And The Stooges records and he hated punk until The Stranglers came along. He played that on his show and another world opened up for us, as it probably started to shut down for him."

Perhaps early evidence of Robert's compulsive nature was that that first Town Hall show was quickly followed by a ludicrously delicious sounding triple-bill of Johnny Thunders and the Heartbreakers, Siouxsie and the Banshees and The Models at Middlesbrough Town Hall Crypt.

He remembers, "Siouxsie and the Banshees were still unsigned and the coolest punk band around. A real force."

Siouxsie, of course, was already infamous after appearing on the Bill Grundy Show the previous December in full Nazi regalia, while Marco Pirroni, later guitarist of Adam and the Ants, was guitarist for The Models at that time.

That same year saw another awesome double bill of The Damned and Penetration at Middlesbrough Town Hall on 17th November 1977. It's worth reflecting that this period was later referred to as the second wave of punk, but that it was only a year after the first wave. It must have felt that every week, when the music papers arrived, things were moving at such a fantastic pace culturally. While it must have been difficult to keep up, musically and stylistically for fans and musicians alike, this line-up of punk pioneers The Damned, plus local heroes Penetration, would be a night that went down in local lore long after the punk dust had settled. Robert and friends had hurried down after school to help Penetration lug their amps up the ramp from Corporation Road into the main hall while lead singer Pauline Murray gave out coveted 'Pauline x' autographs on little shreds of paper.

When I later pressed Rob on his favourite albums of all time, it's no surprise that many are from this era. Anyone who is a music fan will know those life-changing albums from when you are just the right age never leave you.

"Things like Rattus Norvegicus," he says, "but also The Fall's Grotesque After The Gramme (but I could include at least twenty more from that era). Each new Fall album release was a big thing for years. In the Fly Me To The Moon office, we would all gather round a cassette machine and play each new release as it came out. Mid Life Crisis, I particularly loved. And the epic Hex Enduction Hour. The Damned's Machine Gun Etiquette and Damned Induction, PIL's Metal Box… an amazing LP that opened possibilities with Jah Wobble's bass lines, Keith Levine's stark guitar and John Lydon's warbling vocals, as well as The Nightingales' Pigs on Purpose, Iggy Pop and James Williamson's Kill City, Joy Division's two albums and the first New Order album, Funny Times by Misty's Big Adventure, Wire's Silver/Lead, Magazine's Real Life, Punishment of Luxury's Laughing Academy…"

One surmises the list could go on and on and, looking back, it seems 1977 was Robert's musical awakening but he says now, "I don't really play much stuff from the pre-punk days anymore, but it's all still on vinyl in my dad's garage."

3. LINTHORPE VILLAGE, 1986

Middlesbrough Ironopolis Football Club, although only in existence for five years between 1889 and 1893, won three Northern League titles, two cup competitions and reached the FA Cup quarter-finals. The club played at the Paradise Ground, adjacent to Ayresome Park. The club was formed by members of the then amateur Middlesbrough FC, who wanted the town to have a professional club. Ironopolis was accepted into the Second Division for the 1893/94 season. The club lost its stadium at the end of the season. Its financial position was poor, as gate receipts did not cover the cost of player wages and the costs of travelling to fixtures in distant parts of England. In February 1894, all the professional players were served notice of the plans to liquidate the team. Ironopolis resigned from the Football League the following month and folded. Ironopolis and Bootle are the only two clubs to have spent a single season in the Football League.

Fast forward a hundred years and on 21st May 1986, with debts of almost £2 million – a large but not insurmountable amount in the pre-Premier League days – Middlesbrough FC called in the provisional liquidator and by late July, the Inland Revenue had taken the club to court with the judge issuing a winding up order. On 2nd August, manager Bruce Rioch and twenty nine other non-playing staff were sacked and the gates to Ayresome Park were padlocked by the bailiffs and a closed sign hung unceremoniously.

Even at the time it seemed oddly showy for a small town football club as the chains clanged down on the gates, as if they had to secure the stadium in case the entire town forcibly tried to keep the business operational. In my mind, it was one of those padlocks with the spinning cover that drops shut over the keyhole when you take the key out. I remember because my dad had one in his garage. His 'big' padlock.

I was a football mad eleven-year-old in 1986 but yet to fully understand the politics and machinations of a professional football club (even in that era), and I wondered why anyone would lock away something loved by so many. But as dusk took over that day, only a gaggle of supporters and reporters gathered, hushed as if at a hospital bedside. Pan out and, in the surrounding terraced streets, TVs flickered behind net curtains as fathers and sons tuned into the local news… a latter-day Lowry and a tragedy unfolding.

"It was very sad," Rob tells me. "The 80s were a terrible decade in so many ways, I suppose..." as if narrating somebody else's story or recalling something he can no longer quite grasp. It's another endearing trait of his, a misty-eyed melancholy while he often bookends these profound understatements with 'I suppose', a kind of humble disclaimer in case we might disagree with him.

In the days before 24-hour news and social media,

Robert recalls having to wait until a late night news bulletin on Tyne-Tees Television a few days later just to find out if the club had been saved at all.

"You were aware at the time that things were changing," he says, "but we were only twenty eight minutes away from going bust. And that was an era so far before social media and the internet that your only connection was with local radio and television."

Having to wait for the evening news and being so detached from current affairs and local narratives will be alien to many younger readers but this was a time when if a TV show was interrupted for a news flash you knew something really big was happening. Or, if people were huddled around the Radio Rentals window, it was because an aeroplane had been hijacked or another royal engagement or birth had been announced. But the mid-1980s was a time of extreme hardship for many in working-class areas and Middlesbrough was no different. This was just a year before Margaret Thatcher's infamous walk in the wilderness across the demolished debris of nearby Thornaby.

As is usual with these things, it had been a long downhill road for the club to get to this point and it's one that Robert recounts with a stoic realism even now. It is clearly a time that's still very raw for him, as well as for many other fans who still feel betrayed and let down by the powers that be in the higher echelons of the game.

"Looking back now you can trace it from 1981 to 1986," he says. "We got relegated in 1985 and the club's money just ran out. There was hooliganism, the ground was falling to pieces. Bit by bit it was being cordoned off. A terrible decline. And a decline in the town itself."

•

Linthorpe Village, also once known as Linthorpe Lane, was one of a number of hamlets (along with Ayresome and Newport) on one of the main routes out of the settlement of Middlesbrough. The original site nestled between Acklam Road and Burlam Road with the present day cemetery as the village green. What we now know as Linthorpe was one of the original suburbs of Middlesbrough when the town was in its industrial heyday in the late nineteenth and early twentieth centuries as developers bought up swathes of farmland and began to create rows of tree-lined streets of new housing for those benefiting from the steel boom. This new money had also seen the whole town centre relocate, with the building of the new Town Hall in 1889 on the other side of the famous railway line from what would become colloquially known as 'over the border'. It was also the perfect location for newly-elected Football League member, Middlesbrough FC, to set up home.

Ayresome Park was purpose built in between middle-class Ayresome Street and Clive Road to the north and south, and Ayresome Park Road and Middlesbrough Workhouse to the east and west, for the start of the 1903/04 season. In fact, in February 1905 Middlesbrough became the first club to pay £1,000 for a player when they signed Sunderland striker Alf Common. This, combined with the subsequent capture of Derby's England striker, Steve Bloomer, meant that by 1906 Middlesbrough had the most expensive strike partnership in the world at a total cost of £1,750.

Skip forward eighty years, as the gates are padlocked with the club facing extinction, and the area was already a working-class melting pot of chancers, grafters and hard-knock kids kicking balls through the litter strewn alleys with chalk goals and occasional cricket wickets on every terrace end.

The intervening years had seen the club, if not exactly yo-yo, but, move between the top two divisions… at times challenging but never quite meeting their full potential and, at others, languishing nearer the third tier than the first. As cyclical as these things often are, a resurgence in the 1970s was followed by the steep decline in the first half of the 1980s.

By 1986, twenty-four-year-old Robert had already invested a lifetime into his overriding passion but, after attending so many games, he can't remember his exact first match and can now only form an amalgamation of his first ever game some twelve or thirteen years earlier.

"My dad used to take me now and again (my brother was more of a fan than me when we were kids)," he says, "but I remember John Hickton coming off the bench and scoring with his first touch, and me shouting out his name. So, I think it was a 1-1 draw, and I remember where I was sitting in the South Stand."

He remembers that era fondly as a more innocent, trouble free time on the terraces.

He adds, "My brother and me went a few times in the promotion season with Jack Charlton. It was really cheap in those days and that summer my dad got us season tickets and we all went in the East Stand behind the goal. I remember as soon as there was any action at our end, everyone stood up and I couldn't see a thing! That was my first year in secondary school. John Hickton was the first big hero of that time and then Jack Charlton came and moulded the team into his way of playing. Quite rigid but he won the Second Division and set all sorts of records. So that was 1974. And from then on, I had a season ticket for quite a long time. I moved to different parts of the ground but the Holgate end was always a bit scary to me at that age."

I narrowed Rob's possible first game down to a one-all draw against Aston Villa on 24th March 1973 when John Hickton did indeed score the equaliser as a second half substitute, but Rob would later recall a snow-covered FA Cup replay against Manchester City in January 1972, knowing with some certainty that it was not his first game. So, it seems certain that his first game was sometime in 1971 but, more prosaically, less memorable. It seems strange Robert would not have clearer memories of this time. Frustratingly, for all Robert's amazing skills of recalling dates and details, names and faces, it is the early years of his visits to Ayresome Park that are surprisingly scant.

"I saw a couple of games near the end of a season that was ebbing away," he remembers, "possibly versus Cardiff and/or Sheffield United in April 1971, and I do remember liking tricky sub Alan Murray which would have been around this time. And also having to dress smartly. And that my younger brother had been to a match a year earlier… a glamourous high-scoring cup tie too, winning four-one against York City, but not my first game with any certainty, I'm afraid."

Perhaps one minor mystery that will escape us on this occasion.

"I don't recall my first game in the Holgate either," he admits, "but it took me years to get there! I stood in the chicken run on the South Terrace lower section in the mid-1980s with Clem [Mark Clemmit] and probably only graduated to the Holgate properly for the final three or four seasons of Ayresome Park. My friend Julie and I watched John Hendrie dribble through the whole Millwall team before scoring into the Holgate goal from there. I eventually stood with [Bob] Fischer, Stuart [Downing… not that one] and Clem and we even put a spot the ball style cross on a picture of the Riverside of where we wanted to sit – in exactly that same position in the new stadium. I'm still there with Stuart now."

Robert does remember getting sweets on the way to the ground from one of the corner shops on Clive Road, his dad having parked a safe distance away from the ground off Cumberland Road or on Belk Street on the other side of Linthorpe Road.

He says, "If you heard Bernard Gent on Radio Ayresome, broadcasting live from the South Terrace, saying, 'Good afternoon, ladies and gentlemen and boys and girls,' then you knew you were late and needed to get your skates on."

Later on, Robert would pay his fifty pence at the turnstile himself and clamber up the steps to the boys' end, an open-air balcony in the north east corner of the ground. The famous boys' end, the Boys' Enclosure in the top corner of the East Stand, also known as the Bob End where often classmates would stand together, although later many would use its location as a cheap opportunity to jump the wall into the adult section.

In those days, the terraces will have been a formidable breeding ground of young pretenders as the fashions of the day and youthful peacocking jostled with the football for priority, while the metaphorical leap over the wall from the rough and tumble of the boys' enclosure to the real world of the Holgate End where the smell of Bovril and stale fags would have filled the air, in the days before Upex pies and the freshly printed pages of Fly Me To The Moon. It would have been just too enticing for many. After all, who can forget that first crush against a barrier or the familiar surge down the slight steps of the terrace as the ball struck the net.

By 1981, the club was in transition. After Jack Charlton, John Neal took the managerial reins and the club were competitive in the top half of the old First Division, with some good players, until they played an FA Cup quarter-final match against Wolverhampton Wanderers, a match they were expected to win. This was one of Rob's first away matches and he would remember it as – arguably – one of the most pivotal moments in his footballing life.

"It was really weird," he says. "We got beaten in extra time. A real depression fell on the town because we all knew the enormity of that result. We never got past the quarter-finals but we knew that was the end of it and the break-up of the team. It is easy to look back and trace the decline to liquidation in 1986 from that point but while, at the time, we obviously didn't know we were going to almost go out of business, there was a feeling about it as being all or nothing for the club, and, to an extent, for the town. We were a nearly, nearly club. We froze in the spotlights. Others called it the sixth round, we called it the quarter-finals as it was the closest we ever got. This was the fourth time we got to that stage in six years. It was a glass ceiling for the club. We froze in the original game but managed to escape with a draw.

"There must have been ten thousand… coach after coach this time. We queued up, signed up and paid up in a terraced house near Ayresome Park. A young guy took the money, he was so enthusiastic. I found out years later it was Alastair Brownlee. I remember the walk from the buses towards the floodlights on a cold night. The nerves and excitement. Inside, we were in the corner of a giant terrace. The atmosphere was electric. The most amazing night I experienced until the Riverside era. A Bosco Jankovic long shot disallowed and then a goal down. When David Hodgson equalised in front of us, the crowd went wild. I was carried in a wave from near the top to the bottom of the terrace. A long way down and far away from my friends. We should have won but blew our chances to fall into extra time and the shattering taste of defeat. We all joined together singing a very emotional 'We Shall Overcome'. The coaches home were silent. There was a black cloud over the town for days afterwards. I think we almost thought of ourselves as a special club and part of that was the ingrained sense of failure. It rubbed off on the area to some extent. We could lack belief in everything, especially ourselves, because, like the football team, we felt we were doomed, fated. And we were only just entering the 1980s…"

Ask anyone who lived in Middlesbrough around this time and you will get a similar response and, indeed, fans of other clubs even adopt a there-but-for-the-grace-of-God camaraderie towards the sort of misfortune that bestowed Middlesbrough in the 1980s. For a town that prides itself as being the biggest in the country, to be without a football club would have been a disaster and there is still a feeling today that the club was hard-done to by the establishment. Bruce Rioch took over the team again but wasn't allowed to buy any players because the Football League were concerned about letting teams go into administration in case the game got a bad reputation.

"So, unlike everyone else that went bust before us we had to pay off every debt that we owed," says Rob, still visibly bristling.

But this heralded the start of the Steve Gibson era, as he gathered a group of investors together to save the club but, as Robert had told me, "It was actually ICI that saved the club. It was like a company town in a way and [Steve] was really lucky because ICI were contacted and publicly backed him. They just took a punt. So, different groups of people, different companies like Scottish & Newcastle Brewery, all put the money in that the League insisted to guarantee survival… and one weird bloke – a man from Watford who invented self-sealing envelopes – put his own personal money into it. He'd never even been to see the club before. Mossblatt Ex Mill Envelopes. London businessman Henry Moszkowicz. He saw an advert placed in the Sunday Times by Middlesbrough Council appealing for people with funds to help. He had no previous link with the area."

By hook or by crook, it was to herald a new dawn for the club. And the Premier League was just around the corner…

4. EAST BERLIN, 1989

History has remembered the Berlin Wall coming down with images of thousands of East Berliners flocking through the newly opened border to reunite with long lost family, to marvel at Western culture or just to see if the grass really was greener on the other side. But, to one twenty-six-year-old from Middlesbrough, it presented a unique opportunity. By this point, Robert's post-punk band, Shrug, had been going for around four years with limited local success, but they'd been touring the UK, playing with the likes of Canadian post-punks No Means No and Leeds anarchists Chumbawamba. By early 1989, Robert had befriended a Liverpool promoter/chancer who time recalls only as Jim, who had made some connections in West Germany after taking County Durham's Whisky Priests there the previous year. Now, Jim asked Shrug along for a similar tour.

Rob says, "We just rocked up at Checkpoint Charlie with our passports, went through and played this gig."

People tend to forget it was West Berlin that was segregated and surrounded by a wall. Basically, it was a political and cultural outpost of the west in the middle of East Germany that you could only get to through subsidised East German 'Transit Lines'. But, on 9th November 1989, after half a million people gathered on the eastern side in protest at the East German government, the gates were opened and the barrier lifted.

Previously, only major label supported bands, who had applied for visas a year ahead with all sorts of stipulations, had made the journey… Bruce Springsteen had famously performed in East Berlin in July 1988.

Rob adds, "We were on the motorway going across East Germany and we found a radio station and they were playing Shrug and were already talking about the gig in West Berlin."

The band had been talking about things happening in Berlin so they were not wholly unprepared for how things panned out. People were already allowed to travel by train from Poland after the relaxing of the border controls, which was a massive deal for them at the time but nothing like the free movement many of us have enjoyed since. Those lucky enough got the train in but also had to get the train back out on the same day or risk being officially deported.

"When we got to West Berlin," Rob reflected when I first asked him to recount the trip, "there was a massive market with loads of Polish people with tablecloths on the floor selling knives and forks, or anything else they could. It was obvious something momentous was happening, but it was quite sad as well in that respect."

To help us get to this point in the Shrug story, it is worth remembering that in the 1980s it wasn't so easy to even start a band, let alone arrange a European tour. Cheap Eurail passes were all the rage for football hooligans and upwardly mobile students, but not practical if you had three drummers, seven passports and a van full of equipment to get through customs at each pre-Maastricht Treaty border,.

So, let's go back to the start… Robert recalls going to loads of gigs whilst at Leeds University in 1980/81, making friends and contacts. By his final year, he'd already invested in a cheap Yamaha keyboard, which he used to write some 'songs' using autochords.

"One note is a chord," he says. "I was rubbish at that too."

So, when he started thinking about forming a band, it had to be with friends. Enter Sixth Form art classmates, Robert March and Richard Pink.

"We had three songs each – singing our own songs," he adds. "I played one finger keyboards. One night someone shouted, 'What's your name?' and one of us shrugged their shoulders. Shrug was born."

As far as anyone can remember, Shrug formed sometime in the summer of 1985, and Robert, Richard and Robert March quickly secured their first gig, upstairs at The Albert in Middlesbrough. As bands often did back then, they started out drummerless. Taking their inspiration from Mark E. Smith of The Fall, Half Man Half Biscuit and (even if they were yet to know it) Inspiral Carpets, they made do with an out of time drum machine.

After Robert March moved to Leeds to study fine art, they settled on a line-up of Robert, Richard and Kev Wall on bass, before Sarah O'Brien soon joined on keyboards, Ever the contrarians, the band soon ditched the drum machine in exchange for double trouble in the form of Sarah's brother, Richie, "Who we remembered drumming along on the back of the sofa when we were watching TV and we were, like, 'you're in!'. He'd never drummed before!" Sarah's boyfriend, Gary Bradford (percussionist and future Space Raider) completed the line-up. From time to time, the band even had a third drummer in the shape of Carl Sims.

Two other faces from around this time were ROJOR and Michael Baines, who were an integral part of The Albert/Studio 64 nexus…

ROJOR remembers, "The Albert on a Monday evening was a hotbed of edgy creativity. Teesside was awash with cover bands making decent money in Working Men's Clubs but the scene at The Albert was the antidote to stifled artistic expression and the oppressive Thatcherite economics that had hit the North East of England. Monday nights offered original music, new music and new characters. Gigs on a Monday were loud, sweaty and packed. The audience and the bands were the bohemian outriders, the dress code was 'creative', and the music was a fall-out from the punk, new wave-era of the late 70s, early 80s. The PA hammered out noisy guitar riffs. Bands had to hit the ground running to win over the audience. You either went for it and flew high, like Shrug, or you crashed and burned, never to be seen again. Offstage, Rob was always approachable, a charming and humble character.

He was intelligent and I always got the impression he was planning yet another music-based community venture. It was often about watching what Rob was doing to be sure to keep ahead of developments as he was the one setting the direction of travel. As a songwriter, Rob had the skill of telling stories about his world, as well as our local experiences.

"From these embryonic early days came Studio 64. Anyone who was anyone on the Teesside scene recorded there down in the cellars. Descending those stairs was like entering a magical labyrinth. Heating pipes lined the walls and there was no natural light. Most of us in bands were skint and there was no real opportunity to record songs, other than live on cassette at gigs so to have a community space to demo tracks was invaluable. In those Studio 64 days, I learnt so much about sound recording, vocal performance and musical arrangements. Those running the studio were part of the scene and not sneering professional engineers, so we sort of all learned together. Suddenly, recorded music was coming out of Teesside and this gave musicians the chance to send off good quality demos to radio stations and record companies. The current Tees Music Alliance was a natural progression and the success of Green Dragon Studios and the Georgian Theatre owes much to the groundbreaking work of Rob and those early pioneers of the local scene at The Albert."

Michael Baines recalls, "I wasn't part of the steering group that formed to source funding for a recording and rehearsal studio but it was an impressive undertaking, considering they were a group of musicians and music enthusiasts in their twenties or early thirties, with very little experience of applying for such funding, or running such a facility. I think there had been a similar project in Sheffield, called Red Tape Central, that had been a music collective turned studio facility, and that was a source of advice and inspiration. My first encounter with Studio 64 was as a customer booking the rehearsal room in the late 80s. I applied for a place on what was to become an annual sound recording training course, and, on completing the course, was offered a job as a studio engineer, just around the time that the studio was relocated from 64 Corporation Road to further down, opposite Doctor Brown's. There were four or five of us on a Government scheme that was pretty decent, paid a decent rate and wasn't exploitative. When that scheme ended, we formed a workers' co-op, Cellar of Sound, on the Enterprise Allowance scheme, and we were responsible for the rehearsal and recording sessions. An interesting but flawed feature of Studio 64 life in the early days after the relocation was the introduction of night time recording sessions. As electricity was cheaper overnight, it was decided that recording sessions would also be cheaper overnight. It soon transpired that this played havoc with the sound engineers' body clocks, and mistakes were made due to fatigue. Also, bands would book in and embrace the rock 'n' roll cliche of fetching copious amounts of booze to the sessions… only to be too drunk to play, and, in some cases, fall asleep after couple of hours. The overnight sessions didn't last very long, as far as I can remember. Studio 64 divided opinion in the early days but became popular with local and national punk/alternative bands, thanks in no small part to Ian Armstrong, owner of Meantime Records, who would direct the bands on his label to us. It was an almost revolutionary DIY ethic that led to Studio 64's existence."

They were all friends from Middlesbrough Music Collective, and this all mirrored what would happen later with the Fly Me To The Moon football fanzine when Robert took over as editor, in that there were similar collectives around the country. It was a shared underground movement with a DIY ethos, and the collective used to meet in Studio 64 when it was at 64 Corporation Road. They would meet every Sunday, although Rob recalls, "It took me months to speak to anyone. Me and Richard both went there and we eventually formed the band… pretty soon I started putting the gigs on as well as being gig secretary."

The collective were already putting gigs on at The Albert, sometimes downstairs and sometimes up. When Robert took over as gig secretary in 1987, he established Monday night gigs. The night proved so successful, it wasn't long before they were approached by somebody from the Empire pub (now the Swatters Carr… not to be confused with the Empire nightclub on Corporation Road) on Linthorpe Road, which was a much bigger room with a capacity of a hundred.

"It seemed like a lot," he says, "but we moved there and put gigs on upstairs for a few years. It was the only regular weekly gig in Middlesbrough."

From the start, Robert wanted to bring in bands from other areas.

"We all listened to John Peel, so we were aware of lots of little bands" he adds. "I used to go to the 1-in-12 Club in Bradford when I was living in Leeds and that was a collective-run venue. There was a guy there called Nick Toczek, who had this pack that had lists of contacts for press, student radio stations all over the world, booking agencies… it was an absolute gold mine of information. It was a massive thing to have that. So, we started the band and practised in my mam and dad's house and I remember being nervous for a week before the first gig. There were thirty or forty people there but then Robert March left straightaway!"

So, on October 14th 1985 Shrug played their first show, supporting Hold, upstairs at The Albert.

Martyn Hudson Watts remembers, "That early autumn of 1985, I had just started sixth form. The gigs at The Albert were a mainstay… both upstairs and down in the basement. The mission was to get to the gig and get to the bus stop outside the Town Hall without getting a kicking. Unwittingly I found myself, upstairs at The Albert, at Shrug's first gig. I'd seen Rob around at gigs and at Middlesbrough Music Collective, where he always struck me as shy and quiet. Rob seemed excessively nervous but also lyrically and musically totally unhinged.

I caught the name Reg Vardy, or at least I thought I did, amongst the wailing and tempestuousness of that performance. Lyrically, it was like the whole of eccentric Middlesbrough and its characters being paraded before the audience. I was sat right at the front with my mate Dean from school, and Shrug's performance stayed with me. I saw them a few more times over the years before I left Middlesbrough. I can remember being sat in the refectory at university sometime in the early 90s, reading the NME, and there was a review of Shrug, I think at Leeds. To think that of all those bands it was Shrug that got an NME review."

Local film maker Jay-Tee says, "I remember this kind of semi-derelict/sparse/unused small room. I remember seeing Shrug play. They made The Fall look like Take That!"

Fly Me To The Moon writer Chris Bartley kept a poster of that seminal first gig, and was an influential figure in the local music scene at that time. He recalls, "I used to go to sixth form with Robert's brother Stephen, and when Robert finished at Leeds Uni, I was round his mam and dad's house, and I encouraged him to go to Middlesbrough Music Collective (I'd been going since autumn of 1984) so I might have been a very small catalyst of what followed in the birth of Shrug! Ronnie Bur, Richard Sanderson [no relation to Michael] and Steve Weatherall were also regulars at that time."

Shrug of 1985 was much slower than now. And louder… given the number of drummers. Richard had learnt to play as an acoustic guitarist so it was also quite mellow. The Smiths were an early influence.

"Richard and me wrote the songs at first," Rob remembers. "I had shared a flat in Leeds with a drummer who used to play keyboards like a drummer, and I liked that so I started playing my keyboard in time with the drums. Gary was really clever and he liked the fact I couldn't write any music but could make up these tunes that he could then arrange better. Like everyone does, I'd always wanted to be in a band since I was a kid… I used to practise in front of the mirror and all that rubbish."

Musically, Richard had been the driving influence for Robert. "He bought Anarchy in the UK when it first came out and sold it to me for seventy pence. He was into all the pre-punk stuff and we used to go around his house to listen to The Velvet Underground, and Patti Smith. I met him when we were eleven years old. He used to Brylcreem his hair in school and had all these cool bands that nobody had heard of on his haversack. So, he liked everything coming up to punk but then didn't really like punk itself!"

Rob remembers Shrug's first tentative steps outside of Middlesbrough. "Bradford Uni, or the Polytechnic, as it was then. The gig secretary was William Potter, the bass player from Cud. He liked a cassette we sent him and eventually rang us and said, 'I haven't got a support band. I don't suppose you can come… it's tonight.' So, we played with a band called Blyth Power, who are still going today. That was brilliant."

At the time, most bands only played local gigs so it was a conscious decision by Robert and the band to play elsewhere… in the same way it was to invite other bands to come to Teesside. Rob started building up reciprocal exchanges with other collectives around the UK, befriending Ian Armstrong, head of Darlington's Meantime Records, who is still in the music industry today, along the way. Ian had a record label called Meantime Records that he ran from his front room in Darlington. He would bring bands over from North America and balance out their itineraries so they could spend several months in Europe and Britain. Ian's own band was called Dan and, if a support ever didn't turn up in Darlington, then Dan would play. Shrug started doing the same thing in Middlesbrough, and Robert would just drive around picking up whoever was available to play, so sometimes they even played as a three-piece.

"That was nerve wracking," he says, "but you got talking to the other band and they would often ask you to play with them. Michael Baines [who fronted Spit The Pips] used to talk to bands and play all over, but other people didn't really have the confidence at first. Hope Springs Eternal were the other big band of the time and they used to do that as well."

It was through this seemingly random process that Shrug got to be friends with cult Canadian post-punk band, No Means No. After playing with them at the Empire, Shrug were asked to play with them again the following night in Manchester. The Canadians even paid some of Shrug's fee. After that, whenever No Means No came over to the UK, Shrug played with them.

At the time, The Empire had a seemingly constant stream of exciting new bands being booked. "There was an art-core band called The Ex," Rob says, "who were massive in Holland, and they turned up at the venue in a fire engine. Then after the gig, they wanted to know where they could get some petrol, for a fire engine, but the only twenty four hour place was Shell on Newport Road, but I knew they were involved in anarchist demonstrations and stuff and that Shell was a Dutch company. I was scared they might ram the fire engine into the petrol station to make a political statement, but they were actually really nice guys. In the end, they asked us to support them on a tour of The Netherlands."

But the story of the band's apocryphal first European trip started with an EP recorded in early 1989 at Lion Studio in Leeds, which the band had been tipped off about by The Membranes' John Robb.

Rob says, "The EP ended up getting quite a lot of reviews in the national press. We released it on our own Our Mam's Records, partly through Ian Armstrong, and pressed up a thousand copies. I used to give him a lift to Red Rhino distributers in York, so he helped release it through the Cartel distribution network. Red Rhino went bust and a lot of the EPs went missing. So, it was a disappointment but then, sometime later, we put a band from Liverpool on in Middlesbrough, which is how we met Jim so then we quickly recorded an album for the German tour." The band attempted to record the Septober Octember Nowonder – a Laurel and Hardy line – album in one night, for better or for worse… although, in this case, worse, as Robert lost his voice halfway through the session. "We were still getting used to all the equipment – which wasn't working properly anyway – so I had to shout the album because my voice wasn't registering."

To cash in on the German opportunity, Robert also got a run of t-shirts and merchandise produced to make it worth their while. And then, off they went "with the album on vinyl and cassettes… only to find out everyone bought CDs over there!"

And, perhaps a little like it was for The Beatles in Hamburg, Germany wasn't without its problems. "The first gig was in Emden," Rob tells me. "We played for an hour and then the bloke came up and told us to go back on, he wanted us to play 'faster, louder, longer'. He was shouting it from the back!"

The band knew they would have to play long sets but, after playing for two hours on the first night, Robert lost his voice again. After that they played in a tiny squat venue in West Berlin, which is when Jim said he'd been talking to some people, and, it looked like, if they took a chance, they could get a gig in East Berlin…

Craig Hornby, drums, says, "The West Berlin venue was The KOB and we were approached by a guy called Thorsten, from the East, who said he could get us a gig and get us through Checkpoint Charlie. We had to pay a visa charge of 15DM… about £5.50… each. True to his word, the next day Thorsten got us through and it was like stepping back forty years in time. I asked somebody which way it was to the wall and they said, 'Follow the sound of the hammers', which I did…"

Robert recalls, "We didn't see a great deal of Thorsten, as we were only in the East for a matter of hours. But he was a good guy, very open and I do remember him fearing that unification could come too quickly for them in the East. He wanted the pace to slow. I remember him being a very thoughtful guy. I sometimes think about him now and wonder about what happened after. Other people were going through but I'm not sure if we were followed or not while we were there. Possibly… thinking about it now. I'd never been to Berlin before but we knew what we were doing when we got to the East, and we knew their money was only worth a tenth of ours so we filled the van up with diesel and ate well."

The band first went to a top restaurant in the Lichtenberg borough but, as half of them were vegetarian, the East German taste at the time didn't reflect that particular western trend, and they spent ages finding somewhere else that catered to their diets. Had they had stayed in that first restaurant, they might have observed the Stasi building just over the road being raided. They also visited some music shops, as there was already a reputation for good music in the East, and Robert remembers, "We got loads of drumsticks and just spent whatever we could really… we also ended up giving some money away at the venue."

So, on the evening of 15th January 1990, Shrug played Knaack-Klub in East Berlin. Knaack-Klub was a nightclub in Prenzlauer Berg. It opened in 1952 as a youth club before developing into a live music venue where many notable German bands regularly played. Knaack-Klub was like a youth club, or social club for older youths. It eventually closed its doors for the last time in December 2010, a victim of gentrification.

"We played the gig and got fed," Rob says. "It was massive, loads of people there and, again, we had to play for about two hours. Knackering, running and jumping around, just giving it our all… crowd were into it, as well. We shifted some units – as they used to say in those days – and then the van couldn't fit through the alleyway out of the courtyard because it was too high. We had to get loads of people from the venue to jump in the back to lower it, so, by the time we had got out, we'd missed the curfew… we went through late morning and, like Cinderella, had to be back by midnight to head back to the West. We were crapping ourselves but they let us through and I suppose it would have given them more of a problem if we'd been stuck. Then we just went back to our digs in the squat in West Berlin."

A BBC North East News feature at the time saw a young Robert waxing lyrical about the serendipitous events of the tour and his hopes for the future of the band. Looking back now, Robert recalls, in typically Robert style, "Seeing loads and loads of white Trabants, and wondering how you would find your car, but people we spoke to were already worried about the pace of change. They thought it was too fast and they might lose an awful lot and just be engulfed by West Germany. They were quite right, in a way."

Indeed, the West German chancellor Helmut Kohl was keen to take credit for the reunification and, while the East Germans wanted the border open, they didn't want to be suddenly impoverished and second-class citizens. They wanted the West to invest in the East and they didn't want to lose their social provisions, clubs and way of life all at once. Even the dismantling of the wall was political symbolism. There were two walls with a thin strip of no-man's land in between. The west wall was covered in graffiti, while the east wall was a lot more secure, as Rob notes, "These guys were knocking holes in the west wall and selling it for a lot of money. There was an East German soldier looking through the hole with his gun, and we took a photo of that. It became an iconic image – not our actual photo – but we remember the fella doing it and it being this great get rich thing as he sold chunks of it as it went for loads of money. West Berlin was doing everything to attract young people so it had that bohemian capitalist quality, even when we went there to do these small squat gigs."

As a neat little precursor to the long football trips that followed with his beloved Middlesbrough FC years later, Robert remembers having to go through every border to get there. "We had a big carnet in our van with all the gear and had to present it every time but there wasn't always a border guard. Other times, we gave away t-shirts to speed our journey. Once, when we got back to Middlesbrough, we were summoned to customs at Church House…" Robert gestures to the tower block coincidentally next door to our meeting place, "because we didn't have a stamp from one of the borders. It was a big problem all that."

After the Berlin adventure, the band played another venue in Darmstadt in the south of the country, playing two nights that earned them enough money to subsidise the rest of the tour. "The first gig went quite well but the promoter said it was too loud. There were people living next door and he wanted our [three] drummers as far away from the wall as possible. So, the drummers moved to the front of the stage, with me in front of them, and the other musicians moved to the back. It worked so well that we did it for quite a few years afterwards. We played for two-and-a-half hours on the second night, which was knackering. But the audience were joining in with songs they didn't know and we became friends with some who wrote to us afterwards. So, that was our first tour in Europe, but we later went back and played in the Netherlands several times… we had distribution from a label associated with The Ex, which was really good… but it was all people we knew from the early collective days. I've known Ajay Saggar since he was in Dandelion Adventure in the late 80s. He used to live with John Robb but moved to The Netherlands and lived in The Ex's villa, so he's arranged a lot of our tours…"

Ajay says, "It was 1988, I think. I was playing in

Dandelion Adventure, and the guitar player had a solo act called A Howl In The Typewriter. He'd been invited to play in Middlesbrough at The Empire, and asked me if I wanted to join him for the road trip. That's the first time I met Rob – as he put the show on. Shrug might have played that show…. I thought Rob was a really interesting character with a vivid personality. After that, Rob put Dandelion Adventure on and we played many shows with Shrug. In the live music scene in Europe in the 80s and 90s, it was much easier to organise tours and had more to do with a sense of community than money-making ventures. It was very much self-sustained and based on a set of basic values and principles, which most bands understood and adhered to. It was possible to visit different parts of Europe and to build up friendships and connections with people from different countries. Nowadays, if you don't have an agent pulling the strings for you, it's tough to get a tour together."

The Septober Octember Nowonder album itself had been well received in the UK and had opened a number of doors and opportunities for the band to get their name known further afield. Just after its release in 1989, Matt Wells reported in the Gazette that even a penchant for Lowcock's lemonade did not exclude the band from playing a debut London gig in an unnamed pub in Islington. In the same article, keyboardist Sarah was already bemoaning the band's age and complaining they were too old for all that, while there was only a passing reference to the East Berlin show.

A Mick Mercer Melody Maker review in April 1990 described the album as being full of uncomfortable tales everyone can relate to – "where the charisma level never drops" – while other albums reviewed that week were by such luminaries as Bongwater and The Band of Holy Joy. Around the same time, an Everett True – 'the man who discovered grunge' – live review for Shrug's show at the Camden Falcon alongside Sperm Wails and Ajay's Dandelion Adventure, says, "perversely wondrous, Shrug are a sheer delight. Four (yes, f-o-u-r) drummers all pounding to a different beat, singularly ironic keyboards and a singer who possesses the personality of Bruno Brookes and Frank Sidebottom. 'This one's about one of our drummers,' he sneers, pointing out the unfortunate individual, 'it's called Fat Larry's Sweaty Armpits' (or something similar)." He then goes on to compare them to John Peel faves of the day, Yeah Yeah Nor, and I, Ludicrous. High praise indeed.

Another live review from the One in Twelve Club in Bradford, by NME's Ben Thompson, played on similar northern tropes, describing the band as having crawled from beneath the counter of a Middlesbrough chip shop and veering between incompetence, before he namedropped The Fall and Peel again. At times, it's difficult to tell if these are skewed compliments or just the contrary writing styles of the music hacks of the time, especially as a further unattributed article of the same show gleefully reported only fifteen people were in attendance.

However, wherever the band played around 1989/90, it seemed the music press were there to document it. At another show, with The Fflaps at Birmingham Coach and Horses, Adrian Goldberg waxed contentedly about the band featuring, "two drummers [if only he knew!], among a total of six performers onstage, with a seventh member sporadically shaking his maracas at the bar. Shrug unleash a torrent of noise, from which emerges a ramshackle melodic greatness, unduly influenced by the memory of Rolf Harris and the spirit of footer fanzines." And this seemingly unprompted by Robert's involvement in the then fledgling Fly Me To The Moon fanzine. A further Gazette article on 17th June 1989 alluded to the band as perhaps being bigger than The Beatles in Northampton!

As well as the album, there were also several other official – and less official – single releases around this time, including Sir Walter Raleigh's Fast Food Takeover. The band decided to make a video and this is partly where the props the band became famous for started coming in because Robert thought the European crowds, especially, might not understand his accent, even if they did understand English.

"The thing is," he says, "you want to entertain… you want to make an impact and for people to think, 'Wow!'. I used to put Copydex glue on my face and put red felt tip pen on it to be like a zombie guy… with bright hooped jumpers and dayglo fingerless gloves."

The glue on the face was possibly not a great idea, so Robert started to switch to masks and hats. "I collected them or had them made for me. The Three Johns were really into pylons. I told the singer I really would like to wear a pylon on my head on stage. He said let me know if you do. My mate Nigel made it but it was a football floodlight pylon. It was pure Blue Peter stuff… made out of Mr Kipling cake cartons, and it broke on the first night. Chumbawamba always had lots of props and I thought we needed to be quite visual and try to engage with the audience and try and be a bit different. We'd managed to get on two TV programmes in the UK, one was supposed to be national but, at the last minute, it was just local, and the other one was Out of Our Heads on BBC2, where they went out to different regions. We had to audition but it was easy to get through because it was shoegaze time, so all the other bands were looking down and not very televisual. We just played to the camera with all these drummers. We had to sign big contracts and stuff."

The ground-breaking culture show was filmed at Seal Sands and also featured local balladeer Stu Williams, Cleveland Youth Dance Theatre, an Indian dancer called Sunita Sabharwal and Asian artist, Ash.

Rob adds, "We got paid quite a lot actually – in performing rights – which gave us enough money to be able to record and get to gigs and stuff."

It's this kind of make-hay-while-the-sun-shines approach to life that Robert would take forward throughout his life. It was also something that would make for an often rollercoaster lifestyle.

5. SEA OF TRANQUILLITY, 1987

"If I had to fly to the moon, I'd take Tony Mowbray with me. He's a magnificent man."

The moon has long been revered as the very height of human endeavour and, from the Tower of Babel to The Monkey and the Moon, humankind has been fascinated at its ability to always remain frustratingly out of reach. When Middlesbrough manager Bruce Rioch said what he did about club captain Mowbray, it was high praise indeed, and a suitably abstract and in-house quote any self-respecting fanzine needed for a name. So, if 1986 had been an almost unimaginable catastrophe for the club and its supporters, for Robert the aftermath would open up something of an unexpected career opportunity albeit one that took a few years to fully unravel…

Tony says, "I'm conscious of what it's called and why it's [called that] and the connection I have with that. It stemmed from a last-gasp goal I scored in a game. Maybe I had the sort of character that endcared itself to Bruce's personality. When it first started, fanzines were a new development and I think the lads would sometimes sneak a look. If there was something funny in it about one of the lads, it would be all over the dressing room! I'm pleased that it's still going after all this time. It's a credit to the people who have looked after the fanzine over the years, particularly Rob."

I wondered if Bruce also knew the convoluted chain of events he had started with that quote and which ultimately led to this book… in fact, it became an obsession of sorts as I tried to track him down, which was an eventually fruitless chain of events in itself. Now Blackburn Rovers manager, Tony Mowbray lives in Nunthorpe on the outskirts of Middlesbrough, so, enlisting the help of an undesirable local PR type, I managed to contact him, but Bruce was seemingly off-grid. Bruce's son, Gregor, Academy Manager at Wigan Athletic, was an initial point of contact but he had his social media locked down and was reticent… I even tapped up everyone's favourite Boro libertine Bernie Slaven, but to no avail. Now in his seventies, Bruce, a former Arsenal manager and Scottish international, is happily retired and living in Cornwall.

Tony says, "Bruce was the right man at the right time for that football club. He was a disciplinarian but he was a wonderful football tactician who played at the highest level. Bruce left the legacy but the supporters still remember me because Bruce said that if he was going to the moon, he would like me next to him in his rocket ship. But obviously the fans grasped it and it's good for that group of people that the fanzine is still running."

Rob tells me, "There was a fanzine movement at that time. Every club had one. Middlesbrough had two in the early days, Ayresome Angel and Fly Me To The Moon. They were a revolution really."

In the days before social media, mass communication and 24-hour news fans were able to cut out the middleman by writing and publishing for themselves. And they owed a lot to post-punk and music fanzines for that.

"I did that kind of thing," says Rob, as if it was his duty. "I wanted to do a football fanzine but I didn't know what to do. Then Fly Me To The Moon started in September 1988 and I started writing in it fairly early on. There was another guy in charge and he couldn't believe how quickly it grew from a photocopied piece of paper…"

Andy Smelt produced the early editions from his bedroom, meeting people in a Linthorpe pub and "pulled it together like that… he was a printer. Legend has it he did it as penance for once streaking on the pitch as a dare."

Andy says, "None of us had a clue what we were doing with it for the first issue. Looking back, I'm amazed people bothered with it after seeing the state of the first one. It was a great buzz. We seemed to improve it week by week and by issue seven or eight, we were well away."

Colin Hodgson, Tony Pierre and Robbie Boal also helped out in these very early days.

"Robbie's still around," Robert says. "They did it without anybody knowing what it really meant workwise and fairly soon made an error in assuming fanzines should come out every match like programs before they realised that nobody else did that! So, then it had to be a business and there was a few of us that had real input from that point forward."

Fanzines as a medium can be traced back to the 1930s

when political pamphlets and science fiction booklets would be passed around as a way of communicating ideas and opinions. But, look even further back and the penny dreadfuls of the Victorian era, or even further back to very early tabloid reporting which took a very DIY approach to printing and marketing, and it can all be traced forward to the more modern fanzine styles. With the increasing availability of the internet in the late 1990s, the traditional typed and stapled paper zine has largely given way to webzines that are easier to produce and reach large audiences instantaneously.

It was the punk revolution of the 1970s and early 1980s that really relit the fire for fanzines in this country though. Largely marginalised by the broader mainstream magazines, fanzines became a way for the second wave of teenagers to share the latest sounds, shows and fashions. Opinionated often to the point of viciousness, fanzines with names like Sniffing Glue and Vague cemented a subculture that still has undercurrents in society today, such was its bigger cultural impact. Often handwritten or crudely typed with Letraset headers, the zines were then photocopied, with many racking up thousands of sales in the post-punk heyday as counterculture spilled over into everyday life.

Everyone loves an underdog, so it was then only a small leap of faith for this kind of passionate written response to cross over onto the football terraces, as the music and fashions already had and as a natural reaction to the increased commercialisation of football even then.

Then, ultimately, the commercialisation of many fanzines themselves in the 1990s as so-called lad culture prevailed and (true to historical form) another revolution ate itself.

However, for a brief time, football fanzines ruled the underground media as Robert tells me about his particular favourites of this period. "I liked When Saturday Comes. I greatly admired it, still do. It is always funny in parts but also made you think with intelligent, articulate articles. And great cartoons. They had Private Eye style covers and we soon tried to do that. I used to admire another alternative national fanzine called Off The Ball… Adrian Goldberg used to write for them. There were lots of team fanzines that were good. Bradford City's City Gent was the oldest and so everyone followed that. Terrace Talk (York City) and Gillingham's Brian Moore's Head Looks Uncannily Like London Planetarium had a sensational title and was a great fanzine too. I had loads of fanzines in those days. And music ones too. Ablaze was one of many great music fanzines, that was slightly posh, as was Rock'n'Reel a new folk mag that was started roughly the same time as when I was doing music stuff. I think Sean McGhee is still doing it now, thirty-plus years later. You find that fanzine-y people keep doing it. We all admired the fanzines that stayed true to their roots and ethos. They were not magazines but as close to cut-and-paste and for the fans by the fans, with lots of contributors and not one controlling voice as it was possible to be. Co-operatives."

Certainly, Liverpool's The End mixed football with music and fashion. epitomising the terrace culture of the

1980s that Liverpool were arguably at the vanguard of, while Middlesbrough's other fanzine around this time, Ayresome Angel, was a more rag tag operation but one that remains largely enigmatic and is now confined to fading memories, if not the annals of history. Pete Doherty's QPR fanzine, All Quiet On The Western Avenue, took the literary heroism one step further by including hardly any direct football content at all.

In recent years, technological advances have provided broader scope to fanzine making, and savvy editors can afford themselves more upmarket productions while retaining a fanzine approach to content. Boro Mag has recently taken a high brow retrospective approach to stunning effect focusing as much on the photography and a high standard of writing with beautiful results, while Bonkers For Boro is a new fans website and The Boro Breakdown podcast are both fan-led and inclusive… very much in the spirit of fanzines.

But in style, format and content Fly Me To The Moon had settled on something in the more middle ground… Andy had taken ownership but very soon the Downing brothers (Nigel and Stuart) became editors for him. Of course, there were no desktop publishers and PCs at this time so Andy needed all the help he could get, and Robert was keen to chip in.

"A fanzine is a fan's magazine so it's got to be fans doing it," he says. "Not just one fan. I've always stuck to that ethos."

Forming something of a crew, and this being the

graffiti-crazed 1980s, Nigel was known as Endy, and, as well as being exceptional at writing, he was a superb artist and cartoonist. Stuart was known as Miniature G and was the teenage youthful element with a brilliant nickname. But shortly, Endy would go away to be an artist in residence elsewhere and Robert ended up editing for Gillandi (Andy's pen name – he was from Saltersgill). In those days, it was mainly typing up fans' written copy and pulling it together into a magazine… a fanzine was born.

6. YORK, 1985

The Tees Valley can be defined by its greatest physical assets... places such as Hunt Cliff at Saltburn, Hartlepool Headland and, of course, Roseberry Topping. All of which are particularly significant because they represent the many different geological features in the local area... the limestone, ironstone and Jurassic rocks which form the literal bedrock of the area. This underlying geology is historically important, as it was the wealth generated from the mining of the ironstone and its subsequent conversion into iron and steel that founded (and funded) Middlesbrough and many of the surrounding towns and villages through a steel boom of almost unprecedented favour.

Mydislburgh is the earliest recorded use of the name, in connection with a monastic cell in the area dating to 686AD after which the area became intermittently home to waves of Viking settlers, while in 1119 the Church of St Hilda of Middleburg was confirmed near Whitby. The medieval settlement of Stainsby was only deserted in 1757 but, prior to the steel boom, even according to the 1801 census, Middlesbrough was nothing but a small farm with a population of just twenty five people, while Stockton was the main commercial point along the River Tees at this time. Which is what makes the area so historically intriguing, particularly to local historians and archaeologists. By this time, Captain Cook's birthplace on the site of modern Stewart Park (which also hosted Radio 1's Big Weekend in 2019) had disappeared and other areas, such as Ormesby and Tollesby with records dating back to the Doomsday Book, were already abandoned before being subsequently built upon again during the building boom of the mid-twentieth century and are now off-limits archaeology-wise… at least until the land is levelled again.

Extend this process to reimagine the old town of St Hilda's, north of Middlesbrough railway station and all but abandoned nowadays, and you are already seeing the next generation of archaeological sites degenerating in real time. It's easy to see why Robert could easily have been enveloped by the local history bug. In fact, Robert's first proper job was in St Hilda's, where Middlesbrough Council's flagship My Place youth scheme is situated now, the site of the old customs offices. He was a part-time researcher on a local history project in 1984.

"We were researching and then publishing little leaflets on the history of local authority housing in Middlesbrough – a history of council estates," he explains. "Unusual, really. I left when I was offered a full-time post as a 'digger' for York Archaeological Trust, starting in snow and darkness at 8am in a half-demolished glass factory in York. The Site Director, Richard Kemp, sent me off to dig beneath York City walls for a couple of days in a blizzard and find out how stable they were. This was January 1985, I think. I hope I have a CV somewhere in the office because it would be terrible not to have my employment record, such as it has been. It was a very tough intro though, York… I think they were built mostly on sand, so not very stable at all!"

Two days later, Robert was on the main site, the biggest dig in the country, with the aim to unearth Saxon York. "The boss met me and said, 'Right, you will be raring to get going and survey the site.' I looked at him… and you think about all those people that get on by just making it up and pretending… I thought I could. Then I suddenly thought could I hell! I didn't know anything at all about proper surveying. I owned up. He looked livid. But as much as I may have slightly embellished my CV, I had never claimed to be a surveyor. He said I could stay on, paying me £75 a week instead of the £45 a week he was paying some of the beginners, but he handed me a pick axe and pointed at a trench full of concrete and brick rubble that stretched from one side of the site to the other, telling me it was my job to dig it out. It kept me busy for a good few weeks. I originally came back after uni on a Manpower Services scheme and ended up getting taken on in York. I had done a one-day course with a tape measure and a pencil on the moors."

The Manpower Services Commission (MSC) was a quango initiated by Ted Heath's government in 1973. It was a forerunner of the more lauded Youth Training Scheme, intended to lessen the youth unemployment crisis of the time. Think modern apprenticeships as a way to falsify youth unemployment but, for many, it was a valuable bridge between education and employment.

"I thought this guy was a bit of a psycho," Rob says. "I mean, he thought I was a trained surveyor and as a welcome sent me off to dig a hole beneath the city walls in a blizzard. And now he is asking me to clear out a trench that will take me weeks of hard labour. His other party trick was to stand at the main gate with one of those big brick mobile phones and count down the seconds from the speaking clock, as we ran down the road in work boots and loads of layers each morning to not be late. It was like my national service. For six months, it was great though. In the summer I joined another Community Programme scheme in Middlesbrough at Cleveland Archaeology but had to wait a few months before I was allowed to be employed, part-time again. We were playing in Shrug all this time, though. So, part-time wasn't too bad."

However, this inauspicious start in archaeology lit another fire in Robert that continues to this day, and he will often become animated when discussing what is buried beneath us. "I've ended up excavating all sorts of medieval places," he says, "finding things like pieces of Roman pot from France stamped with Made by Patrick in Latin. Amazing."

With a youthful and mischievous bent as to what to do next, Robert enrolled on a History and Geography joint honours course at Leeds University, which built the sort of understated confidence and slight but reasoned gung-ho approach to life that led him to York but would mostly serve Robert well over the years.

"I was into The Fall and The Nightingales," he says,

"so it was quite good to go to university somewhere I knew some of the bands. I used to like The Three Johns and I ended up living in a place with people that knew them, as well as The Mekons and Gang of Four. I was going to lots of underground gigs and ended up getting taught a bit by Jon Langford of The Three Johns and The Mekons on a music course, when he wasn't away playing gigs."

After graduating, Robert lived in Leeds half of the week and then with his parents in Middlesbrough for the other half, on the community work programme, going back and forth when rail travel was still affordable to people on low income.

"I was on the dole for a little bit after finishing uni. In Leeds, we lived in Headingley, and there were always a lot of police in town because there was trouble everywhere. Around the train station, they used to sell Bulldog… NF everywhere, it was appalling. And back in Middlesbrough, there were all these codes like if someone asks you for the time, don't tell them, or if someone has their jacket on inside out it means they are going to hit you. And people used to get beaten up outside Rock Garden because Marimba was upstairs and there was always fighting outside afterwards."

•

Robert later worked for Cleveland Archaeology and then, over the years, assisted Steve Sherlock on a number of jobs. Steve is a revered member of Teesside Archaeological Society, and every year Robert still goes out to an ongoing dig near Ravenscar for Blaise Vyner Archaeological Consultancy on moorland that was almost totally devastated by a massive fire in 2003, that saw more than a hundred firefighters tackle a blaze on four fronts nearly a mile long near Fylingdales. There is usually another day digging for Steve at Street House on the cliffs near Loftus.

"Archaeology is a passion," says Rob. "I have subscribed to Current Archaeology for about twenty five years. I read lots of archaeology and have been digging, mostly badly, since being bought a week's archaeology course on the North Yorkshire Moors for my 21st birthday. Archaeology was my third subject in the first year at university but I dropped it after going on a geography field trip to North Wales. Big mistake. I should have kept on doing it. All the way through school, the three things I was interested in were geography, history and art. In fact, I managed to get them to change the options at Nunthorpe [Comp] so I could take geography and history, rather than one or the other. Anyway, you had to take a third subject in the first year at uni so I chose archaeology, but you then had to drop one of the three. I enjoyed the archaeology course so much and had more or less decided to drop geography but, in the final week of term, we went on a geography field trip to North Wales. Much of what we did there was historical geography and I loved it. So, I dropped archaeology and kept doing history and geography. Geography had loads of early computer programming and data analysis, which I didn't like which, so the archaeology would have stood me in far better stead later."

However, like many of Robert's many other passions, his beloved Boro would inevitably start to get in the way and he would turn down digs in much the same way as he turned down gigs with Shrug. And again, the die was cast.

"I was told at university," he says, "that archaeology casts a spell on you. I think it's true, but I was never very good at it. Steve Sherlock is an incredible local figure for me… from Redcar… and passionate about Redcar, Teesside and indeed Middlesbrough."

Although heading some of the biggest archaeological projects in the UK every year, Steve Sherlock still takes something of a busman's holiday every year to come back and head a band of volunteers at Street House, where he previously discovered the famous Saxon Princess that went on to redefine our understanding of local history and cemented his name in local archaeological folklore.

"It's totally self-funded," Rob explains. "That dig has been massively significant for keeping Kirkleatham Museum, in Redcar, going and putting the town of Loftus on the national map."

Steve and Robert have been friends since the 1980s and have worked together on projects since 2001, but since 2005 have worked on the Street House dig every year. Steve has been an archaeologist for more than thirty years and has spent much of this time in the North East of England, but it was the Saxon Princess discovery that made his name. The seventh century noblewoman is particularly significant as the most northern burial site of its kind and for the quality of the surviving artefacts, some of which can still be seen in Kirkleatham Museum today.

Rob tells me, "I did the whole York thing, then quite a bit of work mainly in Hartlepool. I was based at the Headland, mainly working on digs for Robin Daniels, who later became County Archaeologist for Cleveland and still is Archaeology Officer for our area. We dug a medieval site in Middlegate. It was close to where the original port would have been. It was a real physical effort as we dug a massive hole by hand, deep into the sand until we were certain we were down to a natural level that had not been disturbed previously. On my first day at the site, keen to show that I was a good worker, I swung a pick axe through a water pipe that was supposed to be inactive but wasn't. It went off like an explosion and squirted right into the eyes of my boss. 'That's a good start,' he said, wiping the water away. Luckily he did see the funny side. We looked for an early medieval Franciscan Friary on the Headland, and also tried to find some evidence of an Anglo-Saxon monastery on the site where a Victorian Hall had been demolished. The monastery of St Hild has remained pretty much elusive – it's probably under the present church there – but Anglo-Saxon graves have been found. The Headland is such an exciting area for archaeology. On the dig that happened before my first one there, some medieval leather shoes were found, amongst other things…

"I did some more digging with them at Kilton Castle, a medieval castle that is slowly slipping into a valley not far from Loftus. We uncovered lots of the plan and recorded it so there is a full record before it eventually falls away. Where else? Oh, yes, a dig at a medieval site in a field at Elton, not far from the A66 between Stockton and Darlington. My last projects for them were excavating some medieval remains next to a former manor house in Easington, County Durham, and helping a photographer make a photographic record of another former manor house in Weardale. I kept getting extra time or short extensions to my contract to get to these other sites. Then Steve and I hooked up again and did lots of digs around Teesside, sometimes in people's back gardens before they built an extension. It's interesting. I regret not working more at Loftus where the Saxon Princess was. There are a lot of people there who come to it as a second career later in life, people who joined in the digs then went on to get degrees."

Steve says, "We have a lot in common being Boro fans, as well as liking music, archaeology and local history, and have done some work on excavations on fields and farms around Cleveland and North Yorkshire. Working with Rob is always fun. I always make a point of spending some time digging with him so we can have a good chat. I remember on one job, we each came away with a big joint of meat, because the farmer was so chuffed with the work we had done – which in reality meant we hadn't found much and didn't need to go back the following day!"

Ever selfless, in 2016 Robert even nominated Steve for a local hero award for his work with Operation Nightingale, as well as the Street House project.

Operation Nightingale is a Ministry of Defence controlled initiative that aims to assist the recovery of wounded, injured and sick military personnel and veterans by getting them involved in archaeological investigations. It has been running since 2011 and has undertaken fieldwork both in the UK and overseas. It has helped hundreds of personnel.

Steve says, "Professionally, I work full-time as an archaeologist leading big projects but also have been involved on Operation Nightingale which runs archaeology projects as part of a package of activities to assist with resolving PTSD in service personnel. I lead a project at Marne Barracks in Catterick as part of my Highways England work. After a four-week Operation Nightingale exercise, I did a small follow up job to help a couple of ex-servicemen. We did some archaeological digging at Catterick and I was sitting in the officer mess, trying to get warm and dry when Rob turned up with the people from Teesside Philanthropic Foundation. I was completely shocked, as I was not expecting to see them there, and was then told I was nominated for the Teesside Hero Award by Rob… a most generous gesture.

It was not about Rob or I… the £1,000 from the Teesside Philanthropic Foundation went to SSAFA – the armed forces charity that helps ex-service personnel."

Meanwhile, Robert had been asked to bring two of his passions together and assist with the archaeology on the Breaking Ground project at Bradford Park Avenue in 2015. Rob had been digging with archaeologist Jason Wood and Bradford University students on the old ground of former league side Bradford Park Avenue Football Club, which had unearthed the former goal post holes and even the rusting pegs that held the nets down on the pitch. Artist Neville Gabie, who produced the artwork that today still marks out the old Ayresome Park site, led a team of artists on the site.

"Hundreds of Park Avenue fans returned to their former ground. Very emotional for them," Rob says.

As a result of his involvement in the project, Robert also had a minor part in a book of the dig which went on to make the short list of William Hill Sports Book of the Year in 2017 and afforded him an afternoon reception visit to BAFTA for the finals.

"A posh place and a bit overwhelming in a way," he says. "Our book, Breaking Ground, was totally different from the rest but it was such a great little book that it beat off loads of mainstream rivals to get longlisted and then shortlisted. I wasn't a main writer but was very grateful to be invited along. We thought we might have won but it was not to be… I think we really showed what could be achieved from a community project really firing up the imagination of a community investigating something very special to them. It also showed archaeology and art can work well together and that the past matters."

Robert's dream dig, as you may by now be able to guess, is Middlesbrough, but he says, "They don't have to do any digs in Middlesbrough because the council opted out of their arrangement with Tees Archaeology that used to cover all the boroughs of former Cleveland, due to cut backs in the last decade which means there are no longer any in-house archaeologists watching every development and able to make reports and recommendations which in turn means there is now very limited archaeology in Middlesbrough. But I'm hoping to get heritage or lottery funding to do a dig at Ayresome Park, and I also think they need to do a dig where Digital City is going in because it is very close to the original medieval village."

However, as with everything, Brexit has thrown something of a spanner in the works, although hopefully only temporarily.

Rob adds, "There could be a crisis in archaeology because they are hardly training anymore and the vast majority of diggers are from Europe, which could be affected by Brexit. I did some digging in Wolviston because that was a medieval village too, and there was a development going on at Newton Bewley recently where they dug some test pits but nothing more. One day I hope to help do the dig on the Ayresome Park site. Twice we have been unlucky with funding. It will be third time lucky and it will really excite everyone to revisit the site."

With the area built up, if funding is secured, the Ayresome Park dig should provide a nice return to back garden digs that I couldn't help wonder if Steve Sherlock might come back to help Robert out, adding a fitting synchronicity to this part of Robert's story.

•

In 2009, Robert had run the Middlesbrough 10k race when his friend Sharon Caddell told him about Albert Park Parkrun and another passion was born for him. Parkrun is a collective of 5km events for all-comers that take place every Saturday morning across more than two thousand locations in twenty two countries. First established in Bushy Park, London in 2004 it developed into a network of similar events largely funded by local sponsorship as a kind of franchise with the idea that runners can travel to and then compete in any Parkrun. Of Sharon's involvement in events local to Teesside, Robert describes her as another inspirational figure. She has been Parkrun Director at four different Parkrun courses and has set up three different local runs at Stewart Park, Flatts Lane and HMP Kirklevington. Dozens of runners and Parkrun communities owe a great deal to Sharon and her community spirit, which is seen by many as the key to her success. However, Robert is not quite so fanatical about the Parkruns and admits many Middlesbrough away games have gotten in the way over the years. He did however complete his 350th run on Wimbledon Common in

March 2019 after it coincided with a Middlesbrough away match against Charlton! In fact, the last match before lockdown…

"The course was totally flooded, he says. "At that time, we were more concerned about the weather, which was the same as it is now," as we were speaking almost exactly a year later. "The fans were packed on buses to and from the ground because the train station was closed, and in hindsight it was all a very bad idea indeed. Tragically, a Charlton fan died from Covid not long after going to that game. Wimbledon turned out to my penultimate Parkrun to date. Run 351 was at Tees Barrage the following Saturday. I try my hardest to fit a run in either before I set off or by stopping overnight before and running wherever Boro are playing. I miss all that and miss the friendly group of runners and the café after."

So, evidently Parkruns are still something Robert would like to be able to devote more time to if he could.

At our first ad hoc meeting to discuss the validity of this project, towards the end of 2019, Rob was keen to include members of the community as much as possible and, while it was amazing to be able to get quotes from all the people in this book, including Sharon, it is people like Rosanne and Craig Lightfoot who brought the same café community to Swift Tees running group, based at Hemlington Lake, that underpin Robert's attitude to life and therein his story and are equally important for inclusion.

"It is as much about the tea and cake afterwards as the

training there," Rob tells me. "And everyone is included and nurtured. The priorities are different to a lot of sporting clubs. Everyone tries their hardest but it is about inspiring small steps of progression in newcomers and getting people physically and mentally fit, and enjoying themselves, rather than run times and race wins."

A modest Robert told me how the handicapping system means, "even I have several trophies now with Swift Tees… a 3rd, 2nd and 1st in their seasonal leagues. I'm very proud of them. I have had some bad injuries and had to have a knee operation so I'm just delighted that I can still run at all. I wasn't able to run for over a whole year. A very skilled surgeon saved my bacon. Archaeology and throwing myself around onstage had left my knees in pretty bad shape!"

Sharon says, "After I had my last son, who is twelve now, I saw a sign for Parkruns and went along and fell in love with it straight away. There were less than fifty in the world and Rob and I both have really low registration codes, in the tens of thousands (there are millions registered now). I told Rob he would absolutely love it and helped him register. I knew we had a shared affinity for the park and something that was small, localised and really quite magical, and I thought he would really get that. And he really did, took it on board and promoted it as well."

Rosanne recalls, "I first met Rob through a Parkrun in about 2008 at Albert Park. He's a quiet man but he was very friendly with Sharon Cadell so I got to know him through her. Then he just started coming to Swift Tees and because he has a great listening ear, he just slotted right in. The club is not affiliated. We are a community support group and have raised over £37,000 for different charities across Middlesbrough. Once Rob took us on a run to the place Boro played their first ever match and then we ran back to Albert Park where we ended up having a picnic and recreated the first match, 27-a-side. Afterwards we raffled the match ball for £500. He also helped us arrange the naked Halloween run – not naked, but naked of technology – fancy dress, which suits Rob as he loves dressing up. That started about five or six years ago. Then about four years ago he nominated me and my husband [Craig] to Andy Preston for the Teesside Hero Award and we won £1,000 for Teesside Hospice so that was brilliant. He even used to come to Swift Tees when he was injured just to steward or hand out drinks."

Sharon adds, "He just has this passion for all things Middlesbrough and he will always try and link it to heritage as something to be proud about. He's really connected with Swift Tees as people. When I set up the Stewart Park and Flatts Lane Parkruns, Rob came with me and was there week after week with genuine passions for the sites. Things only Rob would know. He's part of the glue that holds these community groups together."

•

Another thing Robert and I discussed at that fateful early meeting was whether this was the right time for him to authorise and promote such a book, at fifty-nine-years-old, at time of writing, perhaps too young and humble for a memoir and with way too much still going on in his life to almost render aspects of the finished product obsolete before it was even sent to the publisher. Much like with occasional editions of Fly Me To The Moon that were out of date before they got to the printer, but ultimately oversights that shaped the evolution of the magazine and something of a barometer for many aspects of Robert's life. But there was something else that seemed to intrinsically brand Robert's story into the local timeline that serendipitously reared its head as part of Middlesbrough Local History Month in May 2020 and, for me, was the most touching moment of this whole project…

"I do the Local History Month programme each year so I do quite a bit for that and I used to put some stuff in my Gazette column too. I did the Love Middlesbrough blog for years, which included a lot of local history and archaeology stuff. They deleted all my blogs when they updated all the software, five years of stuff. How do you delete stuff online? It's quite hard to do… they even got somebody else to apologise to me," Robert tells me, clearly still foaming.

Middlesbrough Council's approach to culture has not always been inclusive of Teesside as a larger entity and the shared community spirit that exists all the way along the Tees Valley, so perhaps Robert's penchant for advancing his mixed interests towards a common social goal for the wider region was always going to come to a head in the higher floors and plate rooms of the Town Hall in Middlesbrough.

Anyway, Robert knew an audio recording of his grandma existed, partly because his girlfriend at the time, Alison Jarvis, did the interview and gave him a transcript. In fact, he even read from it at his grandma's funeral. Recently, Rob found out that historical researcher and Community Engagement Officer Dr Tosh Warwick was digitising interviews from Teesside Archives' collection from the 1980s and mentioned to him about his grandma, but he thought nothing more of it as life continued to get in the way.

Little did Robert know that Tosh and Ruth Hobbins, also from Teesside Archives, went away, found the recording and programmed it to go online during the month-long virtual version of the annual event.

Rob takes up the story, "Tosh told me it was about shopping and steel workers. I switched it on and hadn't a clue at all. I was gobsmacked. It was an amazing and fabulous surprise. I played it to my dad. Sent it to my brother in Hong Kong and the other two surviving grandkids. My mother would have loved hearing her mam again. It really was amazing, just like my grandma was here now telling me stories as she did."

I had shied away from asking Robert too many probing personal questions but felt this was also the opportune time to ask about his dad's vascular dementia, a gradual decline dementia fairly common in men his age, but very sad, nonetheless.

"He's in care now, sadly," Rob says, "but, yes, he loved the recording of my grandma (my mother's mother) and through that recording I made contact again with cousins in the USA and on the south coast of England. It was amazing to hear her voice again. We both thought so. She had a phenomenal memory and through the recording made in the 1980s, we were able to go back in time to the early years of the 20th century. St Hilda's market, an eclipse, Spanish Flu (she nearly died from that!) and my dad felt upset for my grandma when she recounted a tale of how a St Hilda's market conman had tricked her husband into buying a watch but when they opened the box, they found it empty."

The irony was not lost on either of us that as one pandemic bit hard, Robert had been able to revisit a previous one… albeit tenuously. And what a thrilling artefact through which to rediscover memories of the old town, itself a long-lost artefact.

The circle of life indeed.

7. READING, 1999

If the following years in the Shrug story become sketchier, it's because Robert seemed to focus more on football, immersing himself in the increasingly popular Fly Me To The Moon as the introduction of the Premier League brought a wealth of new opportunities. But then another fortuitous connection presented the band with a gilt-edged chance to make a name for themselves. Ajay did sound and tour managed bands… and one of those bands was American indie-rock legends, Sebadoh. Sebadoh had been formed by Lou Barlow, after he drifted apart from J Mascis in the original carnation of alternative rockers Dinosaur Jr, and pioneered a lo-fi guitar style that helped open the way for bands such as Pavement and Guided By Voices to popularise slacker culture, and cemented them in legend as one of the most influential American bands of all time…

To set this particular scene, in the mid-1990s, Robert had had a bad crash in the band's van.

"I turned it over on the A1," he says. "Destroyed the van."

It was a bad accident that left Carl injured and led to him having physio for quite a while afterwards. Luckily, the rest of the band were just shaken. But Robert lost confidence in driving vans so they didn't do much for a while until they finally got another one for the Sebadoh tour.

Rob adds, "Ajay would organise these tours but then on the night, he would say, 'I haven't got you any accommodation yet, can you announce something on stage'. We usually managed to stay in decent places. We tried to avoid the squats. I always found it strange because people would smash the bathrooms up as they didn't want running water…"

Looking back now, the squat scene was a peculiar subculture that predominated in working class culturally savvy communities across Europe in the 1980s but also one that was peculiarly inclusive in that it allowed bands, artists and, in fact, anyone socially aware enough, to travel the continent at minimal cost in exchange for whatever each had that the other could use. A self-fulfilling, mutually beneficial closed system. Squats provided sanctuary for those who would otherwise have nothing in towns and cities that were also on the brink of social collapse. Abandoned buildings and lives failed, or at least spat out, by society. With the benefit of hindsight, they helped sow the seeds for new scenes to seemingly grow out of nothing. Think of the empty warehouses on the Lower East Side in the 70s and 80s, when New York was threatened with bankruptcy and pounded by austerity. Or Brixton and Hackney in London, where punks and anarchists built a vibrant counterculture to resist the unemployment and despair of Thatcher's Britain during the 80s. Or indeed the East Berlin youth clubs after the border was opened to the more alluring West.

Squatting is a political point, and the art and creativity of resistance often goes hand in hand with that… something we would do well to be mindful of, as a combination of Brexit and the potential loss of venues and adequate housing, fuelled by the pandemic and the government mismanagement of it, might lead to a speedy return to.

Why they wouldn't want running water is still a mystery, though.

So, anyway, Shrug toured with Sebadoh in 1999.

"The first gig," Rob says, "was a big venue in the middle of Brussels. Exciting and nerve-wracking. Sebadoh had a massive student following, but Lou was cracking up a bit because he'd been on the road for so long. He ran off the stage on the first night, saying he was going to kill himself. They had already changed the line-up and had been in Europe a long time. But because we were just jokers, Lou and the others started relaxing and having a laugh with us, diffusing the situation. He really enjoyed it in the end. I went to see him at Reading Festival in the same year because Ajay was doing the sound and I was right down the front. He saw me and started singing a Shrug song, so that was quite good, I suppose."

Ajay remembers, "I was doing sound and tour managing for Sebadoh. I'd worked with them previously and they knew and trusted my taste in music so we got Shrug to come out and play a bunch of shows in France, Belgium and Holland. Wonderful times. There is a live recording from Paris on Shrug's Bandcamp page where members of Sebadoh are singing backup vocals on one track."

Rob adds, "We played some great venues on that tour

and ended up playing in a place in Paris, another place with a limit on the sound, but some guys blagged onto our guest list in exchange for a recording so they gave us a high-quality recording of the gig. Nathan Stephenson was the guitarist then…"

Alas, even by Bruce Rioch standards, Nathan proved difficult to pin down for his memories of that tour, leading me on something of a good-natured, if merry wynd, of texts and promises while mutual friends promised to give him a nudge while regaling me simultaneously about his aloofness and what great stories he could tell me… as I started making mental notes for another book, perhaps. Equally, Richie and Sarah seemed just as keen to stay in the shadows of this part of the Shrug story…

•

All the line-up changes with Shrug might sound complicated, but the only real changes were the number of drummers present and the odd guitarist coming and going… but for a thirty year existence, not a great deal. Guitarist-wise, there was Richard Pink, then there was "a guy called Dale" who still drives bands in Leeds and is a big music character, then Nathan – but he got more into PA work – and then Oli Heffernan joined in 2005, and Richard re-joined the same year.

"So, our guitarists were usually a lot younger… bringing the average age down a little bit!" Rob often jokes, as if addressing the elephant in the room.

Creative workaholic Oli Heffernan has known Rob for twenty years and is a veteran of the Teesside scene where… deep breath… he has played with Idiot Savant, Year of Birds, Houseplants and many more. He records as a solo artist as Ivan The Tolerable, Detective Instinct and others as the urge takes him. He plays, writes and tours Europe with Ajay's King Champion Sounds. He has released music by Gee Gee Alan Partridge, Pellethead and Girl Sweat, amongst others, on his Ack! Ack! Ack! label. Oli also ran a record shop of the same name, has produced gig and tour posters for the likes of Bilge Pump, The Lake Poets and Fret! and, probably for another book, Oli was having a curry with Lou Barlow and Ajay when they heard that Lou Reed had died in 2013.

The drummers eventually wound down to just Richie again, and the best timeline I can make out for the drum stool over the years is: no drummer > drum machine > Richie > Richie/Gary Bradford > Richie/Gary/Carl ("Gary and Richie had an assortment of drums and a table with metal objects and toms mounted on it") > Michael 'Monk' Sanderson > Richie/Gary/Craig 'Weg' Hornby for the first album > Ben Muriel > Richie again.

Michael Sanderson says, "The first gig with drummers was 8th September 1986 at The Albert. It was Gary Bradford and Richie O'Brien. Carl joined for the 13th April 1987 at The Outlook in Darlington, and my first gig with them was 11th July 1987 at St Mary's Centre in Middlesbrough. Not sure when Richie left, but there were three of them for a while between April and July

1987. I only played with Carl and Gary... and for one other gig on 1st May 1988 at Teesside Poly where we had five drummers playing. That was Gary, Carl, Me, Richie and Ian Armstrong (from Dan). My last show was 19th June 1988 at Abingdon Festival where only me and Gary played. Ian Armstrong drummed again on 15th August 1988. Gary's last gig was 10th June 1989 at The Old Vic in Nottingham. For the next two shows, at Parkway Shopping Centre [Author's note: one of which was attended by Robert's parents] in Coulby Newham, Richie was the only drummer (11th and 18th July 89). Craig Hornby was on drums from 5th November 1989 at the Square in Harlow (not sure if this was his first gig or not). Carl started to sing as second vocalist from February 1990, definitely at the Riverside in Newcastle on the 25th. He sang two nights later at the Dovecot in Stockton (upstairs bar) on Scissors and Van With Square Wheels... he climbed up on the speakers and was jumping all around. Great gig. Craig Hornby's last gig was in Cardiff at the Square Club in the spring/summer of 1990."

•

Shrug also toured with New York punks Alice Donut in the early 90s prior to the crash – where a similar pattern had emerged as on the Sebadoh tour, when singer Thomas Antona was ill from touring so Robert ended up singing a song for Alice Donut without even knowing any of the words.

Rob explains, "They had this guy that played the trombone and he used to walk around the venue… god knows what everyone thought having paid all that money. But I guess they were chaotic anyway. Again, Thomas had done a really long tour and just got ill in the middle of it. That was brilliant playing with them, though." Later in our conversation, as if waking in the middle of the night with a sudden revelation, Robert will recall with some clarity that this was an Alice Donut show in Eindhoven, of all places. He knows this because it was when The Fall had just released the single Touch Sensitive, which should give a little insight into the workings of his brain (and his infatuation with the band!).

Unsurprisingly, Robert's other hero at this time was John Peel. Naturally, they had a track featured on the new music champion's Radio 1 show.

"The song was Fear And Violence On The Last Bus Home," Rob says, "and we listened to it round Kev's house. That was about the most exciting thing ever, although unfortunately it didn't lead to the session we had hoped for. But just to hear Peely play and mention us was like walking on air, as well as the airwaves."

Legend has it that Kev still has a tape of the show under lock and key in his loft.

8. NEWPORT, 1994

If 1977 had been a seminal year for Robert musically, 1994 would be similarly so for other reasons. Oasis and Blur were about to storm the pop charts as Britpop swept the nation, and the Taylor Report had revamped and rejuvenated English football as the first season of the Premier League got into full-swing. By 1994, Fly Me To The Moon had a monthly circulation of around 3,500 and Robert was given the opportunity to make it his own when he sat down with Andy to begin what could be described as his life's work.

"In 1994, I bought the fanzine," he explains. "Gillandi was very busy with his screen-printing business but he had some pressure on so I helped him with the finance he needed at the time. We drew up a contract and I set the fanzine up as a company, Fly Me To The Moon 94. I paid a few thousand pounds, I think. We came to a quick agreement, which meant we were both able to concentrate on our different work. Nigel Downing and myself had edited the fanzine for Gillandi for years anyway and been paid by him as he organised the selling of the fanzine. Nigel soon came back from his artist residencies in the Midlands and on the south coast, and between us we found a new office, a starter unit in a Middlesbrough Council office block for the final season at Ayresome Park."

Nigel says, "I'd been co-editing Fly Me To The Moon since 1989, when Rob took over. It was already an established fanzine, but the focus definitely shifted that first season. We looked at what had gone before and thought hard about what we could do to make it a better read. Rob seemed to know everyone and we utilised that to build up a regular group of contributors who established a wide ranging set of features, many of which were of a satirical nature. The visual look was also important. I think we felt very cutting edge using Pagemaker to organise the pages, a big leap from scissors and an electric typewriter. The use of regular cartoon features and my own drawings were a major element of the planning, as were Geoff Thomas's cover images and, later the photographs of Paul Thompson and Tim Hetherington. It was an exciting re-imagining of the fanzine."

Rob recalls, "A season later, Nigel went away again to be an art teacher… and he's been in Somerset for many years now. I am still there now in the same office. Gillandi did well printing and we remained friends. Sharon Caddell helped with editing, proofing and typing at this time and I was lucky to have her really. Bob Fischer came in to do the covers and Donkeywatch, a feature slagging off away players in a playful-ish way. It was this column that caught the eye of the press and he was offered one in a national paper (the Daily Express, I think) for a season. He was like a deputy editor for me for a long time. He must have been frustrated I was doing all the things he was so good at but after his record shop (Yarm Records) he and Mark Clemmit found their radio feet in the back of my car on away cup trips in the 1996/97 season and that kick-started their media careers."

Sharon adds, "I think I was probably quite bossy but unapologetically so! It was a little bit undisciplined. It looked a little bit ramshackle, if I'm honest. His car was full of sellers bags and boxes of fanzines spilling out, and from the state of his boot I just knew his office would be in the same condition and it was… hideous! So, I was a lot more structured and tried to bring a bit more organisation to things and tried to channel their energy more productively. It was quite a competitive environment so I tried to up Rob's game around presentation and to be a bit more savvy about content. We were using Desktop Publisher and learned to use Adobe Pagemaker together and I became a sort of sub-editor, but it was Rob that termed me that. We were really breaking our backs sometimes to get it to the printer and nerves were frazzled, not just between me and Rob but Bob Fischer as well. But it often looked great, neatly laid out and it looked really snazzy. Some really good stuff, when they didn't lose pages between the office and the printers!"

Fly Me To The Moon's starter office on Lorne Street (it seems strange to still call it a starter office after more than a quarter of a century… "It's really small and is full of boxes of fanzines! I'm lucky that it's 24-hour access, which is quite vital really to be able to work on a night.") in Middlesbrough's rundown Newport area reflects the town's odd relationship with its past. Once a bustling working-class residential area, a melting pot of satellite economies of scale and class but largely razed to the ground to make way for industrial units, the absurdly placed bypass and slightly underwhelming edge of town retail. However, it may also seem like the perfect place for this kind of undertaking… in the shadow of the Newport Bridge with the Transporter visible in the distance, and close enough to the banks of the River Tees and estuary that the sense of local pride and historical significance is almost palpable.

Newport Bridge is my favourite of all the bridges across the River Tees, a vertical-lift bridge that stands auspiciously like the Transporter's little brother just underneath the A19 flyover with its more famous counterpart visible in the distance against the backdrop of a sun-splashed estuary – nowadays sans smog – and the ever-cold North Sea. Completed by Dorman Long in 1934, it now acts only as a road bridge in its permanently down position, but it is its predominant twin lifting towers at each end that give the bridge its character. The A19's partner in crime, the A66, cuts a swathe through the centre of town, amputating what is left of some incredible Victorian architecture in Exchange Square, the top floors only visible from the dual carriageway with its odd brick sides as if to stop the cars careering off onto unsuspecting shoppers below. But Newport Bridge, nestled between these two concrete arteries, exudes a stylish charisma … whether it is grey or red, or grey and red, lit up or just subtly imposing in the dark as it has been all of over the years, another benevolent overseer of the town.

In terms of gathering content for the fanzine at this time, Robert explained of his new-found editor role, "In those days you had to do a lot of typing. There was one week where the only way I could do the fanzine was to work for twenty four hours, go to bed the next night and then work another twenty four hours. Six o'clock deadline for the printer. We have used the same printer since the early 90s as well, Pickering Print of Stockton. A one-man band, Ron has never let us down and is a brilliant bloke. It's totally different now though, it just depends how many people send us stuff. I always find that people want to do something every week. They want to do their own features… I live my life around deadlines. I can't do anything without a deadline!"

With this kind of DIY ethos and continual learning curve, it's quickly apparent Fly Me To The Moon is so much more than a labour of love for Robert and a very stressful way to earn a living. He is keen to admit there have been many editorial mistakes with the fanzine over the years, firstly trying to do one every match when others were doing four a season. With this kind of workload, typing up people's hand-written submissions quickly became a full-time job and if each issue sold a couple of thousand that was a lot of money, time-wise, already spent on that, and then there were ill-advised indulgences on things like some of the promotional stunts they came up with…

When Robert first took over the fanzine, he released a single with Tony Mowbray for Tony's testimonial season but Tony got transferred to Celtic just after.

"The tapes actually went to Abbey Road for mastering," Rob says, "but when they went for pressing, they pressed the wrong B-side so they gave me a load of free singles rather than knocking off the price but I couldn't sell them! Records never sound exactly how you want them to (the guy there liked to scratch their name in the vinyl… I don't know if it was Porky but he was one of the famous ones anyway), they had this big massive sci-fi Quatermass mixing desk and played the half inch tape from Studio 64, turned this knob and said, 'What do you think of this?' and it sounded totally different."

The 'Mission From Todd' single was released in time for the last game of the 1990/91 season at Barnsley with all profits split evenly between the Tony Mowbray Testimonial Fund and Studio 64.

Then there were the t-shirts… "There was one with 'Slaven for Scotland' emblazoned on it," Rob says, "but he got picked for Ireland soon after it came out."

In fact, Bruce Rioch himself would succumb to the Fly Me To The Moon curse, being sacked shortly after the team produced a t-shirt to back him in early 1990.

During this time when Nigel and Rob were editors, they did develop an unusual, if mutually beneficial, successful working relationship. Nigel was the artist and Rob was the writer so that already worked well in theory, but they both saw the page differently. Nigel only saw the pictures and Rob only saw the words. However, it did allow them to remain more DIY and in-house because Nigel's cartoons were brilliant and Robert's words accompanied them perfectly.

Nigel says, "In general, we saw things in a similar way, but in the wee small hours and with a deadline looming, I tended to get a bit grumpy. I would go silent on him and just try and get the fanzine done. I think that said a lot about the way that I worked, rather than anything about Rob. There's a great photo – that I think Tim Hetherington took – of us cramped in our tiny office with me looking daggers at Rob. It was like that sometimes, but once the stress of final production was over and the fanzine was safely dropped off for printing, it was all forgotten. We had a lot of fun working together, really. Rob is a really important friend, who is the godfather of all three of my kids… but I never miss that horrible push towards the deadline!"

As something of an aside, I'd heard there was a photo of Robert and Nigel in this office in James Cook Hospital somewhere but it became a bit of an enigma as only my girlfriend (who works there) was able to confirm its existence. However, as luck would have it, Shaun Elliott from Pellethead posted a picture on social media of him posing with the framed picture of a young Nigel and Robert on a wall in the hospital. It looked like it was taken in the early days at the Fly Me To The Moon office, so I eventually asked Robert how it ended up on the wall…

"It was a result of an artist in residency that Nigel Downing did with photographer Tim Hetherington," Rob explains, "in the final season at Ayresome Park, and commissioned by Middlesbrough Council. Afterwards many of the pieces of art and photography were given to the hospital, which must surely be the most viewed gallery in Middlesbrough. We are both really proud and pleased that they can be viewed by people using the hospital. Stephen Gill did colour photos of the Riverside under construction as part of same council project, hence it being gifted to the hospital afterwards."

•

Close working relationships between editor and staff was something that remained long after Nigel had left again, and in 2005 the fanzine even ended up getting voted EMAP Fanzine of the Year, which many would say by that point, and considering everything the club experienced in the intervening years, was recognition long overdue. Robert takes up that particular story… "They never let football fanzines in for some reason, but they did that year and I was invited down to London. They said I had to go on my own so I went down midweek and we won it, Sports Fanzine and Fanzine of the Year. Steve Lamacq was a judge. I was ill, had flu, but I got a magnum of champagne and £1,000 worth of software. It got hardly any publicity locally but I drank as much champagne as I could! It was good to get that recognition, I suppose."

Although Rob tried selling Fly Me To The Moon through a newsagent on several occasions, there was never much appetite for it from the fans. Perhaps, unlike St James' Park, which is right in the centre of town, the Riverside Stadium is a good walk through underdeveloped lowland, and far from the nearest shop despite persistent attempts to regenerate the area.

"We always wanted to stay as a fanzine anyway," Rob says, "and not be a cheap magazine. It took us a long time to even go colour. Our club chairman, Steve Gibson, fell out with me quite publicly for a while because the Sunderland fanzine, A Love Supreme, was being printed at the same printers as the Middlesbrough match day program. He automatically thought these fanzine makers were making a fortune, so he went absolutely wild with me blaming me for everything negative in it."

I think it's worth noting here that during all our meetings and social dalliances over the years, I have never heard Rob say anything negative about the Middlesbrough chairman. Although he did say (and I won't directly quote him here) that an angry Steve Gibson is a formidable sight.

While this little tête-à-tête with the chairman may have been something of a storm in a teacup, it wouldn't be the only time over the years that the fanzine would cause Robert an amount of stress. Remembering the tension of the Juninho days, and in particular the relegation season of 1996/97 when the club had been deducted three points for failing to turn up to a game against Blackburn Rovers, he said he was physically gripped by it, having to do fanzine after fanzine and ending up being quite ill at the end of the season... perhaps similar to those Shrug tours where he was forced to step in for Sebadoh singer, Lou Barlow.

To top it all off, Robert was approached by Total Football magazine to write a big piece criticising the club. The magazine agreed to leave Rob's name off but still pay him quite handsomely for the piece but, common sense prevailing, Rob tells me, "I submitted something... although I wouldn't hammer the club like they wanted me to. But then there was some sort of publishing dispute and it never came out, not in this region anyway. I picked it up at Newcastle Airport a bit later and they had printed my article without a credit, they skewed it and I never got any money. I've always had that loyalty. I took all the fanzine headlines that season from all the local and national publications... lots of ridiculous quotes because the club were in the tabloids, and the mainstream press were homing in on us. The big sports magazines, who were offshoots of Loaded and things like that, had this idea Middlesbrough and Teesside could become the next Manchester. Everyone was firing shots at Middlesbrough as the new upstarts so it was up to the fanzine to keep resisting that so we had things like Graham Kelly's head as the devil. You become quite important when you are doing that kind of thing. It all happened so quickly but then it all fell apart just as quickly."

As with his other passions in life, Rob has built an impressive network of media contacts over the years. Loaded was a ground-breaking if morally dubious 'lads mag', popular in the 1990s with football and Britpop fans alike, while When Saturday Comes was a similarly original football magazine that brought fan discourse to the high street just when the Sky money was perhaps forcing it out of the grounds.

Rob says, "I used to know James Brown actually, who edited Loaded, when I lived in Leeds, through The Three Johns. He just used to hang out at the uni with the bands but Loaded gave the fanzine scene an extra boost in a way. In the late 80s, When Saturday Comes had a list of all the fanzines but it eventually got so long they couldn't print it all because every club had two. Then in the early 90s, there were far less but alternative culture became really mainstream for the first time. When Saturday Comes was upmarket enough to be sold in WH Smith, and I got to know long-time writer Harry Pearson, having read his articles and then his book, The Far Corner, so I contacted him because he was a Boro fan and an extraordinary writer. I admired his work and he made me think and laugh out loud, and I wrote an article for the magazine about bearded footballers and placed an ad for a Shrug record."

Harry says, "I was living in London and used to buy Fly Me To The Moon in Sports Pages bookshop on Charing Cross Road. I didn't know about Shrug. I must have been in the away end at Boro games with Robert in the early 1990s (and maybe at gigs at the Rock Garden long before that...) and travelled to games with Geoff Vickers, Andy Smith, Mike Millet and other members of Middlesbrough Supporters South. They all knew him, but I don't remember meeting him then. The first time I remember spending time with him was when I was doing a signing of The Far Corner at a bookshop in Darlington.

"Later, I guess 1995 or 1996, we did a couple of football writing/comedy events together at The Cornerhouse in Middlesbrough. I have some idea Wilf Mannion came to one of them. The first one was absolutely packed to the rafters. Robert, Bob Fischer, Miniature G and a few others did some sketches and songs that were shambolic and very funny. That whole evening was brilliant and a lot of that was down to Robert. He made me feel part of the town in a way that I never really had before. I saw him off and on at games and around the place after that. I'm not sure about the bearded players article. The first stuff I wrote for the mag was based on my Grandad's stories about growing up in Essex Street and going to Ayresome Park in the 1920s. It was through that I got to know Robert, really."

In 2014, Harry and Daniel Gray (along with Football365's John Nicholson, author of the Nick Guymer novels and another of Teesside's unheralded creatives) held another entertaining discussion on the beautiful game and their writing ahead of that week's Middlesbrough match, and at Robert's request. Held in the Reference Library at Middlesbrough's Central Library, it was part of the wider Discover Middlesbrough Festival, one of Robert's council sponsored events. Rob said at the time, "Although Harry, John and Daniel have given different takes on the game through their writing, they all share a good sense of humour and the ability to tell a story."

Harry says, "The football fanzines came out of punk and they had a spirit of togetherness about them which was really great. Without them, I'd never have become a writer. I know that's true of people who started out writing for Robert, too. That's a big achievement – to give people that platform and the confidence to go on and make a career. He's always been very supportive of the people who write for him, he's too modest to take credit for helping, I know, but he deserves a lot. And I greatly admired his ability always to be in the company of an attractive woman!"

Rob adds with a laugh, "Many of my friends that I went to Boro matches with were females. Sarah from Shrug, we travelled to many away matches together over the years. My friend Sharon worked with me on the fanzine and also went to many matches and met Harry with me. Sharon edited, wrote, type and proofread. Important stuff. She is incredibly smart and is currently studying post grad at Cambridge. I was so lucky… And Louise Wilkin. Harry has definitely met Louise. We have been sitting together at home matches right through the Riverside years (and stood together on the Holgate). She is the most devoted, knowledgeable and supportive person of local gigs I have ever known. Louise works at Arc promoting theatre and getting the public engaged in community."

These days the fanzine is perhaps less reactionary and a more studied response to events on the pitch. This is partly down to circumstance, as well as the evolution of the form, with it having been scaled back to once a month… and if it wasn't for subscriptions, Rob wouldn't be able to carry on doing it.

"It's been a funny thing to do something that has declined season on season since the 90s," he says. "I only print about 300 now and have managed to continue that throughout Covid. I sell as many subscribing as at the ground. But because it was a movement at the end of the 80s, a lot of people who buy, I guess, are people from those days. Dads buy it and give it to their kids and, because I'm selling to them as well, I don't put any swearing in."

This thoughtfulness is something compelling about listening to Rob talk. He always has the best interests of others in mind as the fanzine continues to blaze a trail on diversity issues whilst remaining inclusive and relevant. An issue at the beginning of 2020 was a special campaigning issue around mental health, while another took up the campaign of a group of fans now affectionately known as the 'Boro 44', an example of the selflessness at the core of the fanzine's ethos.

Rob explains, "A group of fans were held by Derby police in 2015 for six hours under a bit of legislation that doesn't require the police to say why they hold people. They needed a lot of money to fight the case civilly so we promoted the cause. They were stopped as they were leaving a pub and held in a church hall, not given any drinks or allowed to go outside for a piss or whatever, and then they were escorted with blue flashing lights to Nottingham Station where they were put on a bus and then taken home…"

It's very rare to hear Robert swear, even mildly, so I could tell that this kind of social prohibition was something that he was particularly passionate about, as he continued unabated, "I get a hell of a lot of trolls on the Fly Me To The Moon website because of my politics. Stuff is allowed on Twitter that Facebook wouldn't allow. Middlesbrough is an area of working-class Sun readers, maybe that explains it. They say I'm a bully and a bigot and they use that to justify it. But it's my website at the end of the day, so if I say someone can't be on it then they can't be on it… it's got nothing to do with football. A lot of my friends have come through the fanzine where they had written first and a lot of writers locally have stayed with the fanzine so it has been quite important, and it is important I retain that position editorially and politically."

Rob is clearly conversant with these modern scourges and it is something that is becoming more apparent as right-wing populism tries to redraw the boundaries on bullying.

"Where do you draw the line on trolling?!" he says. "You will always get people on social media who want to express an opinion and people will always be more anti on social media. Football, politics and everything. It's reactionary. I remember a PR officer speaking to me at Ayresome Park in Robson's first season, I'd been invited to something, and he was asking if I was going to be positive? But I just say what I say. I remember selling a fanzine outside of Burnley later the same season and a policeman coming across and asking who the fanzine was against because the Burnley fanzine was anti-Blackburn… the whole thing! Leeds had an anti-Manchester United one.

"I get grief because I don't call for managers' heads. Maybe when I was younger I did but I think people are too quick to judge. One of the reasons I fell out with the chairman was because I was one of the only people criticising Bryan Robson but I just try to be a bit more measured. Nobody deliberately gets it wrong, I don't think. Look at Gareth Southgate, he's England manager now. It was maybe too much too soon for Southgate. He believed you should start at the bottom as a manager. McClaren made him his first signing and made him almost like a cricket captain so he had that extra responsibility of being like a manager on the pitch, but it was too early for him as manager of the club… he still gets judged on that but he was a young man and people learn. I remember when Mowbray got sacked, we'd played away at Barnsley and it's a ground where you have to walk off at the away end and we'd come back and won 3-2, but the verbal attacks on him as he was walking off were vicious, and he looked up to where we were sitting and I wondered what he was thinking. He'd been the captain fantastic that brought the team back with Bruce Rioch and he was getting all this hatred at him. You need to have some sense of perspective and I wrote about that when it happened to Southgate. You can't be like that."

If this appears at times to be running with the hares and the hounds, it's more because of Rob's deep-seated attachment to both club and supporters than any perceived intention to play both sides against each other. Contrary to many football supporter clichés, Robert seems to manage to remain, in his words, 'measured' and focused on the task at hand while many around him are lost in biased vitriol… a skill any successful editor needs to have.

Despite, or because of this, the current version of the Fly Me To The Moon website provides a modern and functional digital meeting place for fans to converse easily and often. Providing a happy balance of chat, history and a little commerce. For many, it is still the first point of call for club gossip, banter and some quite involved discussions that message boards are still arguably the ideal format for. While the website bears no resemblance to the article heavy approach of the physical zine, the all-inclusive ethos is apparent in the chat streams which are mostly very friendly and civilised these days. Time was message boards had a reputation as a playground of anonymous bullying and, as we have read, that is something Robert has consciously railed against. The website has recently been brought up to date, so for a while there were two message boards, a modern one and a retro one. Two people (plus a third from time to time) moderate the website, often incognito to minimise criticism and trolling.

However, the fanzine has a list of all the contributors, which are usually the same people for the whole season. Rob has made many friends that way over the years. He was lucky during his first few years as editor, in that the technological transformation with internet and emails made life so much easier in terms of editorial efficiency. But, not always one to embrace change, Rob was still pasting some pages up onto A3 sheets until about five or six years ago.

"Bob Fischer and I did a colour cover of Gareth Southgate for the 300th edition," he says. "I was against colour because it was really expensive at that time and we still wanted to keep it as DIY as possible. But the printers started saying they could do it really cheaply and it was just like colour photocopying in a way… that's when we started doing it all on PDFs as well, but still all black and white inside. The thing for us, always working up until the last minute, is the colour cover has to dry but that is a lot quicker now."

Matt Smith, Fly Me To The Moon writer, says, "My first ever Boro match was in 1989 and I've been a regular reader of Fly Me To The Moon since around 1992 so the fanzine has been a part of my pre-football rituals for nearly thirty years. That fact alone seems an incredible statement to write. Rob is the epitome of the 'superfan'.

Steadfast dedication personified. A reassuring constant who, rain, sleet or shine, will be stood in his usual spot, under Harold Shepherdson Way, just past the burger van, politely demanding that his fellow Boro supporters part with a very reasonable £1.50 in exchange for a compendium of scribblings by the likes of me. Rob clearly puts his heart and soul into each and every issue of the fanzine and there must doubtless have been times when he must have considered packing it all in for an easier, less stressful life. In fact, there are times when I struggle to produce eight hundred words of copy in a month, so I simply cannot comprehend the effort that Rob must put in each month just to get the fanzine published. But I'm so glad that he does."

Rob adds, "It's fantastic to still be able to provide a platform for people to write. They can express themselves and write about what they want, not what I want them to write. I mainly do spellchecking now or just ask them to consider a specific word count or a bit of grammar but I'm generally very light on the editing. A lot of fanzines really change and vet articles and change them into a house style. I always had an approach in my head of not being patronising and never deliberately writing in a way that excludes people. Don't use clever language that says this is my discipline, or it can be a problem with language barriers but also with in-jokes that other people might not understand. I don't want us all to come across as smart arses because you used to see a lot of deliberately pretentious writing sometimes."

One of the things that has gone on to define Fly Me To The Moon over the years is its use of cartoons and Rob has always been lucky to have had cartoonists on hand. At first the fanzine didn't have any way of doing photos, being without someone with a darkroom, so they always favoured cartoons for ease. Davey North did Roofus the Boro Dog, and Jack does some simple social commentary cartoons. But other contributors, past and present, are really talented writers. Daniel Gray used to write a column and is now a published author, while Bari Chohan, who sadly died recently, used to submit articles from Kenya and Dubai. Legend has it Bari set up the first nightclub in Middlesbrough and his mother was the first Asian woman to live in Middlesbrough. Bari was also a published poet. Then there is Paul Armstrong, who went on to be Match of the Day editor for thirty years ("the earpiece of Gary Lineker"), who also wrote a number of articles for the fanzine, while recently releasing a book of his own. Paul is something of an outspoken voice himself but remembers those days fondly, saying, "Middlesbrough Supporters South was run by a great mutual friend of both mine and Rob's, Geoff Vickers. MSS's annual do around Christmastime always coincided with a Boro game down south and Rob would stay over in the smoke and come along, then put a write-up in the next Fly Me To The Moon. I'd bought Fly Me To The Moon pretty much from the outset and became a subscriber in the 90s (I still am), so I was delighted to be introduced to the man behind the greatest of all the fanzines. I know I'm biased, but commentators and journalists like Martin Samuel, with no special Boro connections, championed it, especially the genius of Donkeywatch in Martin's case. Rob was probably less bothered about meeting me – since I was known at the time as the 'man who always puts Boro last on Match of the Day'. When I met Rob, I probably went on the defensive and tried to explain that it only seemed that way and that fans of fifteen other clubs often wrote in saying they were always on last too, but it became a good-natured (I think) running joke in Fly Me To The Moon, which I was happy enough to go along with.

"The fanzine is testament to how clever and funny so many people are on Teesside, writing about our shared love for, and exasperation with, our club, and is a great outlet for the typical buttoned-up but literate Teessider. Harry Pearson is the daddy of the modern Boro writers – but Daniel Gray, Bob Fischer and so many others have a beautiful turn of phrase and can be wistful or extremely funny as required. The beauty of Rob's editorship of Fly Me To The Moon is that because it's been so well put together from the early days, the quality is self-perpetuating. The standard is so high, it immediately sets the bar for young writers coming through – and the line between being funny, and going too far and being offensive, has always been set in the right place by Rob. And every season is apparently the last…!"

•

The Boro didn't get very big crowds under the stewardship of Tony Mowbray, only 17-18,000 for his first few games in 2010, but for the fanzine it was a revelation as they suddenly got invited to all the press conferences with the chance to ask questions at the end. In fact, they still get invited now – Robert declined to go in the Gordon Strachan days… "He was just plain rude" – but does go again now.

"It goes TV, then radio, then newspapers," he explains, "so we still can only ever ask one or two questions at the end. It was great attending with Tony Mowbray, with the history of the fanzine, and it has been brilliant Zooming with Neil Warnock. It is a privilege for me to be the only fans' rep present. Warnock even asked me if I could help the fans to write a song for new signing Neeskins Kebano. To his favourite Barry Manilow tune…"

While the Mowbray-era stood out for the fanzine because of the link to its name, the 500th edition was around the same time. Tony had been a big supporter of the fanzine but it became more difficult for him after he fell out with the fans towards the end of his tenure as manager.

Rob says, "It was well past the period when [the fanzine was] seen as baddies and we even had a bit of a reputation for making up nice jokes and being witty, so we weren't seen as so important (or potentially problematic) as the Gazette by then."

In fact, in July 2017 the club imposed reporting restrictions on two of the Gazette's reporters, Dominic Shaw and Jonathan Taylor, preventing them from speaking to then manager Gary Monk during an uneasy pre-season, however these were lifted a year later and they do report again now.

Ever the pragmatist, Robert had realised fairly quickly that if a TV company or advertiser wants some coverage they will speak to the club, manager or anyone with a byline for the on-screen graphics so it has always been quite easy for the fanzine to be visible in that respect.

"There is only one fanzine so they come to us," he says. "It's good publicity but it can cause problems if you are seen as being an unofficial mouthpiece. It's good fun doing lots of interviews but can be quite scary doing a live interview on Look North outside the Riverside when it's fully rehearsed but then just as the interview starts some guy comes up and deliberately puts you off and shouts! But it's been very different since we started doing the fanzine monthly as it's not as immediate, but then social media has become more important and other people have their comments. So, it's more difficult now to make sure the cover doesn't go out of date, which it did a couple of seasons ago when we put Gary Monk in James Cook Hospital with the kids on the cover of the Christmas issue. We printed it on the Friday and he was sacked on the Saturday but we still had to go ahead with it. I've had a few where we've already printed it and the match has been called off. Once we used the same fanzine for the rearranged match and stuck a label over or we've just sold them for the wrong match."

Fly Me To The Moon has been Robert's main income for many years now and I was curious from a business perspective how you monetise this kind of niche project while maintaining the inclusive DIY mentality, and Rob was surprisingly honest and true to his previous assertion that Steve Gibson called it wrong about how much money he was making. It is a heart-warming account of a hand-to-mouth existence over more than two decades that really sums up Rob in a few short sentences.

"Basically," he explains, "you pay the printer, then sell it for every edition. I always wanted to continue it for years and years but you can never look that far ahead. In the old days, the fanzine sold more and was a living but these days it just pays for itself through the adverts on the website message board. That was a bit dodgy during lockdown but [the website] is 24/7, the fanzines are just ten a season. We had looked fairly quickly for an advertiser for the back cover as a kind of sponsor to help with each full season but we have never had a lot of adverts."

For many years Eric Williams was custodian of the back page. "I think he approached me," Rob says. "We had to pay the rent for the office… Nigel and I rented from the council. The council did look after us and you never had to commit much, so it meant we never needed any loans or grants and we could go like that from season to season. It's only in recent years that it has become more difficult with the decline in print media. The peak in sales was actually before I took over. But it went from fifty copies, four pages unstapled to, within a couple of seasons, properly printing… a couple of thousand. It was exciting, a national trend at the time. Every club had one or two. The people doing those fanzines were probably the same kind of post-punk people, so they'd taken something that had always been for a very niche audience to a vast amount of fans so it crossed over in a way it could never have done with music. A lot of the fanzines will have sold more than the club programmes."

While the 600th edition in November 2019 wasn't as big as the 500th, it was still worth celebrating, and as Robert had previously done a thirty-year birthday edition, it seemed to make sense. So he spoke to Generator NE, a business support agency based in Newcastle specialising in cultural ventures, about some crowdfunding but they thought he was better off just funding it via the existing website.

"It's a struggle," he admits, "but, from season to season, it's the subscribers that pull us through and without the website the fanzine wouldn't be possible now."

Even as far back as 2012, Robert had told the Northern Echo that dwindling crowds at Middlesbrough had hit sales of the fanzine and he was considering finishing the print version. However, in the parlance of the day, he was keen to stress to the paper that the website was safe as it was getting "about four million hits a month."

Robert was printing about 600-700 copies at the time but says, "The reaction has been moving. People talking about benefit gigs and subscribing, even though the price of stamps is about to go through the roof, and urging me to keep it going, which is really nice. When you have a decline like that you think maybe it's coming to an end. The club saw the fanzine as opposition for a time but if I ever sold as many as the programme, it was only because the programme wasn't selling many. People used to buy the programme for the team sheet on the back but it was getting increasingly inaccurate and there was very little information of any interest inside. Then there was a middleman with the journalists that were writing in the programme and that was what we were cutting out. If you go back to the 80s, the programme was terrible and when we started it was only two years after the club had gone bust, but we were always doing something different to the programme."

Fly Me To The Moon started when the club were in the old top flight and were getting twenty-plus thousand for home games, but the club lost the first match the fanzine came out (1-0 against Sheffield Wednesday) then got relegated. The crowds didn't really return until the move to the new Riverside stadium.

Rob says, "We didn't know how many to print, we didn't know where to stand because the roads were still being built around the ground. So, we printed 2,500 as a total guess. Gillandi said that was too many, and he was right. We had sold an awful lot for the last game at Ayresome Park. But it sold really well for that season generally."

Speaking just before lockdown when the club were perilously close to the relegation zone Robert was equally open with me. "I think if we get relegated this year, it will be quite hard to continue the fanzine… maybe just as a subscription. There are only three of us selling on matchday now anyway."

I was shocked by this revelation and realised how attached I had become to my adopted home town and how ubiquitous the fanzine is, even to those with little more than a passing interest in the club, but it made sense, given the potentially catastrophic reduction in matchday attendances that a drop into League One would probably bring.

As something of a comparison, another North East club struggling with poor results and reduced crowds were Sunderland.

"There aren't as many subscribers as the Sunderland one, and the Newcastle one is sold in newsagents. People don't buy things in newsagents as much here. Different cultures for different places. With Middlesbrough having a local owner, the ethos is more about [reinvestment and sustainability] whereas it could be seen that I was taking money out of that closed system. Stoke's fanzine, The Oatcake, was a good one and we were always vying with them. I think they were the first to fifty issues and we were the first to a hundred. We beat them to two hundred and two hundred and fifty issues then they raced us to three hundred… in fact, they got obsessed by it. They were working out how and when they would overtake us, looking ahead at all the fixtures. So, at the last minute I pretended we were going to print one for a reserve game just to put a spanner in their works and tease them. It wasn't true. The Oatcake sadly ended back in 2019... was run throughout by Martin Smith. A life's work."

But, Rob's proudest achievement was being able to produce editions for cup finals and other big occasions, which was always hard because it's more difficult to get permission to sell at a neutral ground. However, there are plenty of souvenir requests and the local printers are usually pretty flexible around this kind of event. Robert produced one for the UEFA Cup final (of course he did) and funded it with adverts. The flight operator ended up paying for most of it, and Rob and his small cohort in Eindhoven just walked around giving it to people for free. He also produced some t-shirts that he managed to get sent over with the BBC team and then sold them to help fund the following season.

"We did two cup finals," he says. "League Cup and FA Cup. One of them was A4 size." Proud as punch of the special editions. "Nigel, Stuart and I always dreamed of doing a summer special but never knew how to sell a holiday fanzine, but we did do an annual in 2000 and 2001. A proper one with a hardback." And, in fact, the Official 'Unofficial Middlesbrough Millanual' (actually published in 1999, if the title is a little confusing in hindsight) is still available at time of writing on Amazon for a princely £4.99.

Robert preferred to take the pre-season off though, to indulge his other passions... to go digging, get a job or "doss around or whatever". When the fanzine was being produced for every home match, it was a lot of typing and hoping people submitted on time so it was a full-time job, and then in the week up to printing he would work overnight, get a few hours' sleep and then complete production the next morning… this would be every two weeks. And he always managed to do it.

"Before Ron Pickering," he says, "it was almost in-house. We would finish up, go off to the Havana or Arena and then come back at 3am and start helping put it together. We were able to push it to the limits. The sellers would be coming in and we'd still be putting it together."

If all this sounds fantastically carefree and a little gauche that is because it was, but Rob never lost sight of the business in hand.

He adds, "People say it wouldn't have lasted this long if I hadn't taken it over. Before I owned it, I used to help with putting it together. I introduced them to someone who had a very early desktop publisher which cost £10k. It didn't look like any kind of desktop now but just being able to do that… you try to be reactionary at first but then try to become part of people's matchday habit. People still tell me they have to buy the fanzine off me or we will lose the match."

It is perhaps a bit late to bring a geography lesson to the party but Rob will be a familiar figure to many. You'll find him on the corner of the car park if you approach the stadium from the south west corner, either along Windward Way from the Cineworld underpass or via the Six Medals pub from North Ormesby.

"Going back to the Bryan Robson era," he says, "we didn't have that good a relationship with the club. They would probably let me sell it in the car park now but it pays to stay independent and that's what we're all about. We had a one-way argument, I suppose you could say, with Steve Gibson and he's a bit sort of scary when he's shouting at you, but that mellowed. When a club is not doing well, it's fashionable to be disdainful towards the owner but I've still got total admiration for what he's done. He was wrong to argue with me at the time as he'd been given some wrong information but it's in the past. He still puts as much of his own money in every year as he's allowed and people still say the club are ripping the fans off…"

Through all our conversations, Robert is most animated when talking about the fans' relationship with the club and it's clear he has the club's best interests at heart throughout.

"Through the fanzine," he says, "I'm part of the supporters forum and we meet the supporters every month and try to be a conduit and present ideas to the club."

In the modern game, for a club consistently in the higher echelons of a billion pound industry, it's impossible to overstate the importance of Robert's little cog in this monumentally big wheel.

9. MIDDLEHAVEN, 1995

With Middlesbrough FC and its supporters galvanised in adversity after their brush with liquidation before the start of the 1986/87 season, Rob set about attending as many games as possible just as the latter part of the 1980s became synonymous with pitch invasions and hooliganism as English fans became the scourge of Europe in the eyes of the government and mainstream media, and as fan safety seemed to become a secondary concern to crowd control.

Ayresome Park was one of the old breed of modular football stadiums – a new stand here, an extension there, get in as many as possible – grounds that had developed character over decades as the congregation ebbed and flowed in size.

"People get very misty eyed about it," he says, "but it could be bleakly cold and empty."

Ayresome Park itself had remained relatively unchanged since 1903 but had started to become recognisable as the ground many fans will remember with the building of the new South Stand in 1937, while, for the World Cup in 1966, the East Stand was covered and four thousand extra seats added. To use a religious metaphor, they were churches, but scatter-designed like the gallery motifs of Whitby's famous St Mary's Church on the cliff-top, but with standing and seating, and toilets open to the elements.

"Middlesbrough were quite visionary building the new stadium [when they did] but it was sad [to leave Ayresome Park]," Rob says. "With seated stadiums you can tell when they are empty much more. You can't tell as much if there is a thin spread on a terrace, but you can see seats. You'd get some quite small crowds at Ayresome Park where it didn't look as empty, but when it was full it was ridiculously full." An observation that would become particularly prescient when clubs briefly trialled returning socially distanced crowds to the stadiums at the start of the 2020/21 season.

However, years before the Hillsborough disaster, many of the old grounds had become dangerous places for large crowds of people to regularly congregate. An old friend of Robert's called Jean, who contributed to Fly Me To The Moon until her recent death, had been in a crush at Bolton's old Burnden Park ground as a young girl just after the Second World War when massive crowds were the norm. Thirty-three Bolton supporters were killed and hundreds more injured, but it wasn't until the 1970s when there was a much worse accident at Rangers' Ibrox Park when dozens of fans fell down a flight of steps, resulting in sixty six deaths and hundreds more injuries, that it was taken seriously as a problem. For anybody not used to football crowds in those days, you would regularly see hundreds of people moving together on the terraces, like waves of grain or a wave breaking along a shore. Bands of men. At Ayresome Park the year after it had hosted

World Cup games in 1966, the club got promoted and 40,000 plus were in the ground at times.

"People used to say that as kids they would get a 'squeeze' and be lifted over the turnstile so they weren't counted so God knows what the crowds really were," Rob says. "At one game, there was a surge and an advertising hoarding collapsed and many people ended up on the pitch and everyone just laughed about it. There could have been loads of people killed. Before Hillsborough, we had already done something in the fanzine about the dangers of the fences because during the Bradford fire disaster in 1985, people escaped from the fire onto the pitch so people started questioning the perimeter fences then, like if something happened where would they go?"

Crowd management theory at the time meant small pens and paddocks were popular, partly as a way of stopping the hooligan element from roaming the stadium, looking for errant away fans, and as a way of limiting overcrowding. It had previously been common for stadiums to have huge greyhound stadium-style circular terraces with seated stands above where necessary. It was similar to the races, hence the term paddock was popularised. Robert was not a fan. "They used to have razor wire and spikes and all sorts," he says, "so not at all like the races, more like a prison. There was that brief era where they divided terraces into pens and you'd fill up one pen at a time so the people in the middle were part of that big atmosphere and you and I could stand at the corner where it would have been half empty. It wasn't about safety it was about crowd control. It was horrendous really."

There have been numerous books by alleged ex-football firm members keen to make a quick pound from their take on terrace culture and the football train shenanigans of the day, but true to himself, Robert's version of the fabled away days of this era is refreshingly but typically realistic and sanguine.

"I didn't go to loads back then," he says, "but we went to Stoke and the train was even slower than the mail train. The slowest thing on the rails, it would take hours. Inside the carriages were just wood and then you got to the station and were marched from the station through the town and people were jeering at you. It was a weird experience."

Of all the away trips of this era, and any era come to think of it, it was one peripheral London club with a particular notoriety for hooliganism that earned themselves a reputation as one of the most disliked clubs in the country, and Robert is not afraid to pass his on opinion on Millwall…

He says, "You've got your own station there, in theory anyway, so they just take you from the station through this metal cage to the ground. We played there with Tony Mowbray as manager, so not that long ago, and the atmosphere… there was an offside and their fans were already winding themselves up and it must have been the last straw. They just started throwing things on the pitch and I looked around and saw all these blokes in their sixties with their kids, three generations sometimes, trying to get on the pitch. All the players had to go off. They came back on but it was a hostile environment and the sort of thing that is just not allowed anywhere else…"

•

After attending Ayresome Park for over twenty years, Rob attended the final match there on 30th April 1995… a vital 2-1 victory over Luton Town in the penultimate game of the 1994/95 season before the club went on to secure the Division 1 title and promotion to the Premier League a week later away at Tranmere Rovers. Before the match, a who's who of club legends were paraded around the pitch before the Riverside Stadium name was revealed for the first time. In usual Middlesbrough fashion, a hard fought John Hendrie double on the day just about secured promotion to the Premier League in front of the home support so, in many ways, a fitting farewell for the fans used to emotional turbulence.

One can imagine a typically masculine grief as the whistle blew at the old stadium for the final time, though it must also be noted by this time, league football, at least, was already a lot more inclusive but, still, after nigh on a hundred years of blood, sweat and tears, it's easy to see how religious and battlefield metaphors drop into use so easily when it comes to describing football stadia. So, the rusting turnstiles creaked shut for the final time and the last roars from the crowd drifted off down the steps to the terraced streets outside and dissipated in the breeze like they had never been there. Walk those streets now late on a quiet night and some say you can still hear whisps of commentary and rustles of chatter, even a padlock being unlocked…

But times change and things move on and for Middlesbrough FC it was time to move on. The old ground was demolished a couple of years later, although the same gates that had been locked only nine years earlier were transported across town to take pride of place in front of the new West Stand as the club started the next Premier League season in their new Riverside ground.

Going back to 1988, there had been a broadly positive feeling amongst fans as the club had been promoted from the old third division and then got promoted again but they weren't able to sustain the regeneration because the football league had been so hard on the club to deter others from thinking administration might be an easy option. Chairman Steve Gibson was not happy about having to pay off some of the outstanding debts to former directors, and the crowds in that first season had been tiny so the cash was hardly flowing.

Rob takes up the story… "Even for Bryan Robson's first season at Ayresome Park, there were a lot of crowds under 20,000, which was quite sad really, and people have such a nostalgia for it but the whole thing cranked up when it went to the Riverside. Andy [Smelt] said that when everyone went to the first game they were swan-necking and we felt like we were walking to Wembley. A fully enclosed stadium, not like a ground. We couldn't believe it. They did quite a bit of work on atmosphere, acoustics and being close to the pitch… and they had fans going out to Millwall, as they were the first new stadium and it was like a factory, soulless. Sounds awful to say but there were a lot of lessons learnt there. And then Sunderland and Leicester learnt from us…"

In a further personal twist for Rob, in 1997 he became the first person to sign up to purchase one of the new properties on the old Ayresome Park site, and Robert's house now is just off the pitch… roughly where the boys' end was… where he would pay his fifty pence every other week when he was growing up, and now where he has lived since the houses were first completed in the year 2000.

"I can see the penalty spot," he says, "because it's marked by a brass football on the ground."

Developers Wimpey and Middlesbrough Council had worked with artist Neville Gabie on his Trophy Room commemorative art project that sought to incorporate artworks in and around the new development as symbolic allusions to the past usage of the land and repurposing by remembering.

Rob adds, "At that time, there was an initiative called Percent for Art where councils could say to developers that they had to give a percentage of the money to pay for something creative. I was involved with Cleveland

Arts in choosing an artist and in the end it was between two entries. One person wanted to put a giant rattle but Neville's was kind of archaeological in that he marked different parts of the ground that tell the story that you can piece together as a map. Since then, and partly because of that, I've shown people round from Australia and South Korea, a guy from Aldershot and, in 2002, the North Koreans came round to my house… the survivors of the 1966 World Cup squad that played at Ayresome Park."

Famously, Ayresome Park had been chosen as one of two North East grounds to host group games at the World Cup in England and would put on one of the most famous upsets in World Cup history. The group consisted of USSR, Italy, North Korea and Chile with the ground hosting three games. The USSR beat Chile 3-0, and Chile and North Korea staged a one-all draw. But it was the final match that would be remembered down the ages. With other results going in their favour, a draw would be enough for Italy in their final group game at Ayresome Park against the North Koreans. Nearly 19,000 fans in the ground, including nearly 3,000 Italians saw the favourites reduced to ten men after thirty minutes due to an injury (no substitutes were allowed in the tournament) and the crowd could sense an upset when Pak Doo-ik put the underdogs ahead just before half-time. It was a long second-half as a resolute Korean defence held out for the win in the match, while also winning over the Middlesbrough crowd…

So, almost inevitably, the one about the North Korean delegation, a foreign spy and an MI5 agent…

Rob remembers clearly, "A film crew went out to find the team and arranged for them to come back to Middlesbrough. They wanted to come back because of how well they were welcomed here not long after the Korean war. I watched them walk down the road in their red tracksuits with the film crew and the news travelled round the world. A few years later, Middlesbrough ladies went over and played in North Korea and that led to reciprocal invites. Neville pressed a football boot into plaster of Paris and that denotes the point where [Pak Doo-ik] scored the goal that knocked out Italy… and the North Korean authorities had declared it a piece of national heritage, the only one outside of North Korea, so they all gathered round it and sang a song. When the North Koreans last came, they invited a South Korean ambassador and they all met at a match at the Riverside… which was a real diplomatic breakthrough (although I think they fired a load of missiles a few weeks later!). There was a North Korean spy and somebody from MI5 and they had to stay in twos so one was always watching the other one. A couple of years after the women went over, I showed another delegation around the Ayresome Park site. It was kept quiet and it turned out the person I had shown around was the Foreign Minister of North Korea. Two years after that, he rang me up on my mobile and asked me for a phone number for the women's FA, which was really weird. He said who he was and reminded me about a friend dropping a camera on the ground as we toured the ground as he chatted to me from Pyong Yang... it was all quite surreal."

Incredible and unlikely anecdotes aside, this continued dedication to the heritage of the club and the geographical preservation of past glories and ignominies is commitment personified, and the idea that Rob still gets up every morning and throws open his curtains to see the old penalty spot marked out on the ground is an image I can't shake.

Other clubs have done similar things to mark significant sites. Arsenal's old Highbury ground embraced the fact that some of the building and facias were Grade II listed by redeveloping the stands into luxury apartments, while the pitch area has even been retained as communal gardens. However, Robert's one man commitment to maintain the Ayresome Park memory rather than reimagining the past as part of something more modern is something unique and to be applauded. As a new chapter (literally) was about to begin for the club when the Premier League money started to flow only ten years on from almost going into liquidation, the club found themselves as one of the most exciting prospects in the country with a high-profile manager in the dugout and a number of marquee players on the pitch, as well as some often unwanted tabloid attention...

10. CARDIFF, 2004

At the time, 1996 was considered something of a cultural high point. New Labour were about to sweep into power on a weird wave of nostalgia for the kind of narcistic, misogynistic politics deemed the zenith of post-war euphoria. A sweet spot somewhere between June and July 1967 that only really existed in the drug-fuelled fantasies of those too stoned to remember it. But, the new money of the Premier League and the Rule Britannia hijacking of Britpop by the tabloids had seen the Spice Girls and Noel Gallagher oddly positioned as pillars of the community and meant, for an equally brief period, London, and, by proxy somewhere along the line, Middlesbrough became the place to be. Bryan Robson had been unveiled as Middlesbrough manager in May 1994, which was a coup in itself, and some would claim the capture of Robson as manager is the club's greatest ever signing. But it was Steve Gibson that followed through with a further injection of his own cash for players to match the manager's stature and meant by 1996 Middlesbrough were one of the most exciting prospects in English football and set off a chain of events that would last well over a decade for the club…

Supporting any club is a tragedy of sorts, but for Middlesbrough fans the highs and lows take on something of a Shakespearean comedy. All fans like to see an underdog do well, such as when Leicester won the Premier

League in 2016, or when clubs like Huddersfield Town or Sheffield United hold their own in the Premier League, or even Liverpool and Man United's dramatic comebacks in Champions' League finals but, truth be told, most fans never get to experience that kind of unrefined drama first hand.

"Obviously I've been to a lot of football matches," Rob says. "I don't know how many. I should sit down and work it out. I'll have been to over a thousand."

But when I ask Robert about his favourite match of them all, I'm not surprised by his response…

"I suppose the last five minutes of Steaua Bucharest [at the Riverside]. The impossible was happening and everyone was just screaming, there was an almost primal reaction. And winning the League Cup. People sometimes forget we did win a cup. I remember after the final everyone just sitting there in shock. People didn't believe what had happened. I actually know some people who said they'd stop supporting the club because now we had actually won something! Before the game I went round all the bars and people were optimistic but kept telling me it was our last chance."

The negative attitude was partly because the club had lost so many important matches in the preceding years and people were afraid of being let down again, but Robert had been to Bolton the week before as part of the press build-up and they were so annoyed at the ticket allocation, he had an inkling about the big day.

"Middlesbrough fans were there early, the day before,"

he says, "and went down to the stadium. I was at both ends of the pitch because I was doing Sky TV stuff and the Bolton end was just so quiet. And, on the day, we were 2-0 up within ten minutes and that was partly down to the fans. Bolton were just not ready for it in any sense."

Indeed, the League Cup Final of 2004 at the Millennium Stadium in Cardiff, while the new Wembley was still under construction, was arguably the high point in the club's history. However, by going two goals ahead within seven minutes of kick-off before consummately seeing off a 2-1 win to finally win the club's first silverware after near misses under Bryan Robson in the FA Cup in 1997 and another two previous league cup finals in 1997 and 1998, I wondered if even the most passionate supporter might admit to having something of the edge taken off the whole experience. I've also wondered on occasion if the fact that it wasn't played at the traditional home of English football at Wembley might, in some way, tarnish the achievement, or if it would have become quickly overshadowed by the European runs of the following two seasons… though a succession of play-off finals also meant the club would also visit the so-called hallowed turf.

But, if there has been an occasional anti-climax over the years, the greatest night the Riverside has seen in its short life is undoubtedly the UEFA Cup semi-final in 2006… a night which had all the drama, the angst and the elation that all great cup games should have. After losing the first leg away 1-0, the club went a further two goals behind in the second leg at the Riverside before Maccarone clawed one back just before half-time, leaving an unlikely three goal comeback in the second half as Viduka, Riggott and another Maccarone strike sealed the victory to conjure those immortal words from local commentator Ali Brownlee.

Rob says, "I remember sitting in a club somewhere in Cardiff and watching this big screen as the coach was leaving on Sky and I rushed out of the club and down to the ground, got filmed and then taken into the ground, filmed on a seat and then went back into the club… and all these people pointing at the screen and then pointing at me in disbelief. That sort of thing was fantastic. Sky also liked to put somebody on with a byline, so as a fanzine editor I did loads of that sort of thing in those seasons. Coming back from the dead twice after having already been to the away legs and seen the holes we were in. We went to Basel in the quarters and we came away 2-0 down at the end of that and they did a lap of honour, that's how certain they were. At Steaua Bucharest, the fans came out celebrating in the streets as if they had won after that match…"

Robert is very much the antithesis to the terrace lad (or lass) and embraced the broader cultural opportunities these experiences allowed alongside the football itself so each new European away game presented itself as an entirely different sort of adventure which, although they could get a bit hairy at times, were for the most part broadly positive experiences.

"That was incredible to go to that city [Bucharest] and see Ceausescu's palace," he says. "It was very partisan. We had a Romanian film crew that came with us and to the hotel, just trying to film as much as possible. There would be another club in the city wherever you went and Inter [Bucharest] turned up and there was some sort of factional rivalry. I don't know why. We struck up some amazing friendships during that period. The first game in Europe was Ostrava and this guy got in touch with us through the fanzine website and said 'How can I help?'."

He had hired a bar but realised the fans didn't know what they were getting themselves into so he hired students as ambassadors for the city and, in fact, Robert has still got some of the t-shirts they wore. Ahead of its time in public relations terms, especially in football. But it didn't end there either, he then went on to book a hotel out for Middlesbrough fans and somehow organised many more tickets than the initial 1,000 allocation for fans.

Rob adds, "Phenomenal amount of money he must have put up, just a normal guy who worked in IT or whatever. He was called 'Boro Miro' [Vladimir Janak to his teachers] and years later he emigrated here, having stayed friends with a few people and having organised a couple of football tournaments to stay in touch. He eventually came over here to work…"

Miro himself says, "I support Banik Ostrava Football Club and since 2004 I support Boro as well. I remember I met Rob in Ostrava in one of the pubs on Stodolni Street, which I managed to book for Boro supporters. My first contact with Boro supporters happened on the Fly Me To The Moon message board. Later I discovered it was Rob who was running that message board and fanzine. In 2004, just after they won the Czech football league, Banik decided to take their old website down without first launching the new one. I wondered how Boro fans would cope with that lack of official information and I felt ashamed for such an ignorant approach from my club to Boro supporters. That's why I decided to help. I registered on Fly Me To The Moon and posted my offer to help. In the first hour, I had received fifty email messages. I tried to answer them all but then got another hundred new emails. So, I decided to set up a website for Boro fans and I started to post articles with advice on how to get to Ostrava from Prague, where to find accommodation, how much is food, transport, and so on. Whenever I posted contact numbers of some hotels, they were fully booked in minutes.

"Some fans messaged me and asked me to help them with the Hotel Metropol where none of the staff could speak English. I went there to check the situation and unfortunately there was really no one speaking English, so I booked the whole hotel on my own and made a deal with hotel owners that I'll bring my own staff in once the Boro fans arrived. It was a huge risk for me and my family but the story had a happy ending. Many fans flew over to Katowice airport and the only reasonable way to get to Ostrava from there was by coach. So, I hired three luxury coaches on my own and sent them – each with two girls, members of Miro's Boro Embassy Team – to pick the fans up and get them to Ostrava. Miro's Boro Embassy Team was a bunch of fifteen people who agreed to help Boro supporters during their stay in Ostrava. I split them into smaller groups and sent them to the railway stations, bus stations and airports as coach stewards, and of course to the Hotel Metropol. I made a great deal with one of Ostrava's taxi companies so every time anyone from Boro needed a taxi, Boro Embassy Team called the company and the price was always only £2.30.

"Unfortunately, some of the Banik supporters are known for their violent behaviour in the town before and after the game. I wanted to make the stay safe for all Boro supporters so I contacted the toughest core of the hooligans. They agreed to meet me and they even agreed to take a part in a fans' friendly match I organised to build some bonds between both sides… it ended with a six-all draw.

"Middlesbrough only got nine hundred and fifty tickets but it was clear there would be about three to four thousand supporters traveling to Ostrava. I met the Banik officials and tried to convince them to extend the away sector. They refused my plan, explaining to me that the change (moving barriers etc.) would cost them £4,500. My attempt to convince them that the extra fans would be happy to pay £5 more to cover it wasn't successful. After that, with the help of my Boro Embassy team, we bought a few hundred more tickets. Even after more than fifteen years, it's still a massively emotional experience for me. People in my country for many decades used to call Ostrava the steel heart of the Czech Republic because of so many steelworks. Later, most of them were shut down and abandoned. Sound familiar? After all I did, the fans invited me back to Middlesbrough and our story about a friendship between rival fans became interesting for the media and Anthony Vickers from the Gazette, but then it went crazy and Sky Sports wanted to cover my stay in Middlesbrough!

"In 2005, I organised a fans' rematch in Ostrava. About ten Boro lads came over to take part and spend a short holiday in Ostrava. Then in 2006, my family spent our holiday in Middlesbrough and we played another rematch. It was our best family holiday ever. All the time we felt so welcome. At that time I made a few real friends here and I'm happy and grateful I can still call them my friends today. And I deeply fell in love with this country, with local people, with Middlesbrough and, of course, with Boro."

While Miro's account is certainly extraordinary, it was by no means the only show of generosity and benevolence as the club explored some of Europe's less well travelled incredible city culture.

Next up for Robert was Graz.

"A beautiful city," he says, "and there was a guy there called Tomas who gave us a choice between a glass arc in the middle of the river with surround windows or an Irish bar, so we said we'd better do the Irish bar! I travelled there independently via Vienna and he called me up… he'd booked this bar and was offering guided tours around Graz. Amazing people. He also invited a group of us to the training ground to meet all the players before the match."

Rob's long-time friend Geoff Vickers would organise a lot of the travel at this time and a company called Flight Options, who do football travel, contacted Robert the summer before the first European season and offered to be the advertising conduit for fans.

"They were incredible, miles ahead of all the others for football travel," he says, "and they flew out of Teesside Airport too. So, the airport was packed for all those trips and they also knew about all the problems with hooligans."

Geoff says, "Rob was brilliant at forging contacts with opposition supporters groups and Graz was an excellent example. He started up correspondence with the president of Graz supporters' club, and, when we got to Graz, he met up with us for a beer in the evening and the next day, the day of the match, he invited us over to the Graz club's training HQ to meet the players and have lunch. This made these trips special."

Paul Armstrong adds, "Rob had contacted their fans in advance and somehow he and Geoff were invited to lunch with the Graz squad at their training ground. My wife and I missed out on that, but after a 2-2 draw in the sub-zero temperatures of an Austrian February we found Rob, Geoff and about twenty locals in a classic bierkeller with oompah music, massive steins of beer and currywurst. I was due back in my office in London the following afternoon, after an early flight via somewhere in Germany, and turned up at work in a sorry state after an unexpected night on the tiles with complete strangers who'd somehow become Rob's best friends in the course of the trip."

"When we went to Zante," Rob says, "the club didn't put on any transport so Geoff organised everything and it took us two planes and a train ride through the night to get to Zante. It was brilliant... the European years... you saw all these places you would never ever go to and have great experiences. There were some throwbacks to the hooligan days because there were some idiots who were attracted back into it – and some nasty enclaves abroad too – but, by and large, we saw some fantastic places, great atmospheres and unbelievable cup dramas."

While in the UK, the overt hooliganism, street fighting and terrace violence had all but been eradicated after the Hillsborough disaster, elsewhere in mainland Europe this wasn't always the case.

"Going to Rome was terrible," Rob remembers, "absolutely appalling. I was called in as fan rep to be told the match plan was we had to stay behind for two hours after the match for them to disperse all the home fans. We all had to meet centrally, every single fan, and be coached to the ground because it wasn't safe to walk. We had just beaten Roma, they were top of Serie A, and we were eventually dropped in a park in the middle of the night. Rome is fantastic but there was an election on and there were posters of Mussolini's granddaughter just outside the hotel. I still find it perplexing. Hitler's name was deliberately eradicated, the last relatives took the decision… but, anyway, one of the bars we had been told was safe to use had been attacked by Ultras when they knew that the police shift was changing. We were all searched on our way into the ground, lipstick taken off women and stuff but the Ultras had weapons and were firing coins across glass partitions in the stadium…"

If there is anything Robert remembers from these times, it's that there were many more positives than negatives in Europe and it was an amazing opportunity to be able to support your team. "Sitting in a café the next day somewhere like Athens and looking in the paper through all the other big names in Europe and wondering where you could end up next in your part of the draw was amazing. That season was phenomenal. The final… yeah, we played a fantastic team and we always managed to win against the odds but looking back some of the players that played for Sevilla were just too good for us. We had chances but… after a hell of a lot of games. We beat Stuttgart, who'd won the Bundesliga a couple of seasons before and had a really top team, and Roma had been on a record-equalling unbeaten run. Two really, really good sides to beat in that run."

In front of 36,500 fans, the final itself had been dominated by Sevilla after they took a twenty-seventh minute lead through Luis Fabiano, who headed in a Dani Alves cross. Even though they had to wait until a seventieth minute strike from Enzo Maresca to double their lead before he scored a second six minutes later, Frederic Kanoute rounded off a consummate looking 4-0 win. But just reading the names of the goal scorers aloud underlines just what an accomplished Spanish side Middlesbrough were up against that night in Eindhoven… what was not to be, was not to be.

Rob also remembers coming away from the Eindhoven game and seeing Tony Mowbray, of all people, outside the stadium on the way back to his coach. Robert recalls they both felt very empty as the club had lost, comprehensively in the end, and had lost the manager too, to England. The pair also wondered where the club would go then as they had a lot of older, expensive players and fans had not exactly been flocking through the turnstiles for most of that season… it was doubtful the club could sustain player wages. And they were out of Europe.

"I hoped Mowbray would be our manager one day soon. That would be something to look forward to," Rob says and recalls, "Flying back from our Rhineland base the day after the night before with my dad on the plane, organised by Flight Options the tour organisers that Fly Me To The Moon worked with, we were all really disappointed. We'd more or less just landed at Teesside, I turned on my phone and Talk Radio phoned me. As soon as I got home, they interviewed me live, Adrian Durham, and he led with the line that Boro had lost because our fans had all been drunk whilst Sevilla supporters got behind their team all day and built a formidable atmosphere. I was shocked. I hadn't seen that coming at all. I told them we lost on the pitch to a very good side. Having followed my team all round Europe, sometimes taking planes, trains and automobiles, I didn't need some professional media radio presenter preaching to me about who was a good or bad fan. I was not impressed. Back to earth, back to reality."

Rob had sold a few 'Lightning Strikes Twice' Eindhoven t-shirts but had given away a lot of fanzines that had been for advertising so had a bit of financial work to carry out back at base, but he doesn't recall now what else he might have done to keep him occupied that summer.

"Maybe went to see my brother in Hong Kong," he says. "The good thing about fanzines in those days was that you had a bit of time off. And after that season, going all over Europe and all over in the FA Cup to the semi-final, we all needed a rest."

And, all good things must come to an end, so a month later, Robert was in a small crowd at the unveiling of Gareth Southgate as the club's new manager after the departure of Steve McClaren to manage the England national team.

Outside the Riverside Stadium, Steve Gibson stepped across to ask Robert what he thought… a sure sign that any previous tensions between the pair had vanished.

"I had a lot of admiration for Gareth," Rob says. "I once had to look up a word after interviewing him as a player to check I knew the meaning. That doesn't happen often. Never. Gibson then explained how he had considered a former Bayern Munich manager, he didn't say the name, but explained how it was Gareth who felt right."

•

It's amazing for any fan to experience the highs and lows of cup runs and big one-off games but they are fleeting memories, and what all fans really want is for their club to sustain a level of success. In terms of full seasons, Rob remembers the 1996/97 season, with Bryan Robson in charge when the club got to the League Cup final and then got relegated, as incredible. To use a popular metaphor of the Britpop-era, it was like a goldfish bowl with all the media interest in the club and the phenomenal number of games that they had to play.

Brazilian star Emerson had walked out after a couple of months and everything was very high profile, with certain elements of the media seemingly obsessing about a perceived upstart club seen to be buying their way to success, the same way Blackburn Rovers had done a few seasons previously after signing Alan Shearer, and they were shocked that Juninho had come to a club like Middlesbrough.

"He should have gone to Arsenal really," Rob says, "but, like Bryan Robson coming, a new stadium (which looked like Wembley when we first saw it), and getting into the new Premier League and with a current England international in Nicky Barmby, we were living a dream, so the whole stadium was immediately sold-out when Juninho came in October."

Echoing when he found out the club had been saved from liquidation, Robert remembers he was in Kwik Save when he heard the news the Juninho signing was confirmed.

Rob adds, "I still think he was the best player in the world for those two seasons. And then getting Ravanelli as well, who had just scored in the European Cup final to clinch the cup... I became friends with his cousin. Even Emerson was an unbelievable player in the first few months. He reminded everyone of Graeme Souness when he was at Middlesbrough... how he was so strong and held people off. So those three and Barmby and Craig Hignett. It was a phenomenal team but it had weaknesses at the back and we lost a lot of games. To get to the cup finals... but then with the three-point deduction that led to the relegation meant in the summer, we just had to get rid."

Not one to look a gift horse in the mouth, Robert, in an Independent article around this time, espoused on all things Robson in an early clickbait style (ever the visionary). Even if the article was a little disparaging in comparing Juninho to Andy Peake! However, in typical Rob Nichols fashion, Robson gets a few backhanded compliments, "...even though he doesn't live here." While some of the lower profile players get a welcome pat on the back so... "young Ben Roberts, as he's known", Curtis Fleming, Neil Cox and Clayton Blackmore all get the Nichols thumbs up. Media opportunities are something Robert has always had one eye on, and he even got into bed with

Steve Gibson's old nemesis, The Roker Report, in 2017, for an interview about Aitor Karanka and then-caretaker and ex-Sunderland player, Steve Agnew.

It's interesting to hear Rob still talk proudly of walking up to the Riverside for the first time. As one of the first new build stadiums in the wake of the Taylor Report, after the Hillsborough disaster, it was something to be proud of. There was , as there still is, much talk of developing the area around the ground, and some of Robert's recollections of that time will be all too familiar to many.

"There was a big political thing between Middlesbrough and Redcar & Cleveland councils as the land was dual authority at the time. It was Middlesbrough, then it was English Estates, then it was Teesside Development Corporation whose idea was the club would get the ground as the centre of a big development. One of the reasons that didn't happen was because they couldn't build a supermarket... and the reason the supermarket couldn't be built was because Asda at South Bank objected. That news came through when we were on the coach to the League Cup final. And you see it to this day with the aborted Sainsbury's unit. Middlesbrough College was built with a street running through it and the idea was that there would be shops and cafes. They built that one Community In A Cube tower block with the houses on top and the idea was that they would build right around the dock area but during the recession they just upped sticks and went back to London."

The Corporation were widely criticised for leaving a legacy of inappropriate and threadbare developments while, at time of writing, the Sainsbury's development is still mothballed with the future of high street and instore shopping looking more precarious than ever. Similarly, the fabled snowdome development, which would see the biggest indoor real snow centre between Castleford and Glasgow, stretch from the Hydraulic Clock Tower to Temenos, where Ali Brownlee's words are immortalised in brick, has also been abandoned as financially unmanageable.

Apropos, on Ali Brownlee, Rob says, "He was a very nice man… very passionate and a great spokesman. If Alastair Brownlee thought something was good and said that to you, you thought, 'Ah, that's brilliant'. He always wanted to help the fanzine. He liked the Roofus the Boro Dog cartoon and we'd talk about that."

Rob has used his influential position to act as a conduit, or a go-between of sorts, between fans and club over the years, and even now there is still a fans representation every month that Robert attends where he can talk to senior people from the club and try to influence policy as much as possible on behalf of the fans.

"The Football Supporters Association recognised us as one of the best in the country," he says. "You don't get involved in the team or any big financial decisions but the ticketing and pricing is the main point of contention at the moment. We continue to argue with them, particularly around teenage concessions. I've been face to face with Neil [Bowser] the Chief Exec on the matter and he showed me the Financial Fair Play handbook, which is huge, so they are genuinely complex negotiations."

This position of responsibility does also afford Robert the opportunity to represent the fans in all manner of ways not always widely known and it's always nice to hear him talk fondly of these occasions, even if the circumstances are sometimes unfortunate. Alan Keen, who was a Labour MP for Brentford, died in 2011 but for twenty years was also a Middlesbrough FC scout, and at his funeral, Robert had the honour of being the supporters representative and stood up and gave an address. What Robert didn't know was who else would be speaking beforehand. As it turned out it was Ed Miliband, the Labour leader at the time, while Neil Kinnock was also in attendance and said "smashing" to Robert afterwards, in his inimitable Welsh drawl. Robert also got to speak to Gordon Brown.

"It was sad," he says, "because Alan was such a nice guy, but it was incredible to be in that kind of company. Thank God I didn't know in advance!"

However, for all the ups and downs, all the happy and sad occasions, it was the club's move to the Riverside Stadium that history (or perhaps Wikipedia) will remember of this period in a hundred years' time.

"I used to stand in the Holgate end at Ayresome Park," Rob says, "which was the popular end behind the goal, so when we were invited to apply for tickets for the new stadium, a group of us got together, and they gave us a map of the new ground and you got to put an X, like spot the ball, where we stood in the Holgate, and that's where we got our seats behind the goal, near the top, in the middle. There are less and less of us each season now but there are still some of us from that original group. It used to be the noisy end but they built up the facing stand, the South Stand, and that is where Red Faction are now."

And that, in a nice and unexpectedly touching moment, is the essence of Rob's story. While everything has changed and grown around him, as it does for everyone, he has embraced it all with a remarkable and unflinching grace and poise, confronting all the challenges and opportunities life has thrown him, while also quietly managing to stay the same.

11. STROMNESS, 2018

Shrug had wound down again in 2002, as Robert explains, "We had done a free gig at the Cornerhouse pub for my fortieth birthday, we had loads of people there and I think we just thought we would pack in."

But in 2005 they got invited back to headline John Peel Day at the Georgian Theatre in Stockton and, unable to turn it down, they were seemingly reinvigorated with Oli on board and Richard back into the fold as guitarists. To put things in context, the band celebrated their twentieth birthday week in 2005, bookended with a Fall support slot and the headline gig at John Peel Day. Quite the celebration. However, the Guns N' Roses-esque recording pace, would mean it would still be a further fourteen years before the band released second album, Island Complex.

"The Fall didn't know anything about it. It was The Fall and John Cooper Clarke and another band, who cancelled, so the manager of the Town Hall, a woman called Pat Fysh, rang and asked if we fancied playing because she knew I loved The Fall. It was really last minute so we just turned up, and he [Fall singer Mark E Smith] didn't soundcheck anyway so he wasn't there. That was in the Crypt.

"We played with the Buzzcocks once in the Crypt as well and that was an experience. Their sound guys wouldn't let us use microphones on the drums because they wanted the Buzzcocks to sound better. So, we had two drummers, no microphones and we weren't allowed to use certain settings. The band themselves might not have known. That wasn't that long ago either. Afterwards someone came up to me asking if we wanted to play in Manchester, but could we cut out all the silly stuff. I told John Robb and he thought that was hilarious. We never played covers and always tried to sound different right from the very start, partly helped by the fact we couldn't play any music and just wrote silly songs!"

Robert explains the decision to bring Oli – the best part of twenty years younger than the rest of the band – into the fold at this time. "In the early days, me and Richard wrote it all. Richard wrote the music and some of the lyrics as well. But Oli wrote most of the music for the new album."

The process was really quick again once the decision had been made. Oli had always wanted to do an album although Rob was initially reticent, partly because the band hadn't made a full album for so long. Oli put most of an album together online for the rest of the band to see how it could work, while Nigel Crooks from Teesside University was already desperate to record an album at his Goosed Records base. So, Oli went away and wrote most of the music and Robert took a writer's trip to Orkney and wrote most of the lyrics on the ferry. They recorded the majority of the album in one go again.

"That was really important," Rob says. "I went back over the lyrics and gave them a sense of wholeness and inserted stuff to make it timely and some other stuff to do with Brexit and islands and local folklore and shifted them around a bit. There is also a couple of links with the first album, if anyone ever got that."

One of the album's biggest influences was Amy Liptrot's book, The Outrun, which explores the badlands of addiction through the winds and wildness of Orkney, and mirrors Robert's interest in local folklore while also directly reflecting where the lyrics were born. The Teesside link also prevails in that Captain Cook's ships, Resolution and Discovery, stopped at Stromness, on the return leg of the explorer's ill-fated trip to Hawaii, as crewman returned what was left of their captain's body to Britain. The cover of the album depicts the English coastline, overlaying a famous picture of Cook on the Hawaiian beach about to be killed.

"His remains were not returned in Hawaii..." Rob says, "except his hands and some bits of flesh that were buried at sea. Not a nice business."

Stromness is today the sort of far-flung desolate beauty spot perfect for a staycation of reflection and solitude for those of a certain age, or maybe an inspirational setting for a book or lyric writing break. One can easily imagine Robert hunched over a desk in a threadbare room, pen in hand as the waves crashed below with the ghost of Cook at his shoulder. Back then, as the travel-weary Resolution and Discovery came over the horizon, they would have been met by a humble, if strategic, fishing outpost for whaling fleets dealing in Inuit and Arctic artefacts, a far cry from the Kealakekua Bay beach where Cook had met his untimely death a few months previously. The image of the cavalier captain on the beach is a contentious one. Is he beckoning his men to come forth and engage, or holding them off in an attempt to disquiet a potential situation with the indigenous Hawaiians? Either way, it didn't end well for the intrepid explorer during the ensuing skirmish as he was stabbed and died. The overlay of the two images on the album cover is one that might not immediately slot into the longer Shrug story but consider the band's forays into eastern Europe, Robert's penchant for the wilderness of a rural dig and the ghostly/historic imagery that often inspires his lyrics and you get a feel for the subtle depth of influences that powers the band.

Of the album Robert would confess, "It was good that Oli forced us to do it. I probably should have promoted it more. It's the pre-order thing now I don't get. I didn't even get a review of the album in NARC Magazine because I didn't think about it, I didn't know how to do it."

Of course, work and family commitments did sometimes get in the way. Or, for Robert, football. So, often, recording sessions were squeezed in where they could fit and promotional activity was limited to a quick interview in the pub after work or a late-night flurry of emails to radio pluggers and promoters. But with Oli on board, everything seemed unusually organised this time around.

"We rehearsed," Rob says. "I threw in some tunes

and then we supplemented them with a couple of old ones – we had Whitby Kipper and a couple of other kipper songs... don't know why they are called that. I thought after all these years if we do an album it has to be a whole thing and of the moment, not just bringing together thirty years of back catalogue. And that is what we did, we recorded an album with some spirit, verve and meaning about islands, folklore and living in the edgelands of pre-Brexit Britain. And it was such a thrill to get interviewed about it – after all those years – and to hear people saying they enjoyed it. I just wish I didn't have so many of the records still in my spare room! Vinyl is nice but it's bulky to store."

Oli says, "I first met Rob around 1998, when I first started playing gigs. I used to send him CDs and letters all the time for him to review, basically just hassled him to death, like every band in Teesside during those pre-internet days! I used to see him at gigs I went to and, once I discovered we both had a mutual love of The Fall, I used to scrounge a lift to see them every time they toured. One of my first Shrug gigs was supporting The Fall in Boro Town Hall... that was a good one! I originally joined just to fill in for Nathan for a few gigs he couldn't do in 2005 but then I just never went away. When Nathan came back, we did some gigs with three guitar players.

"I think I ended up writing the bulk of Island Complex, mainly for the reason that I'm really fast and we didn't have very long to do it. Nigel asked me and it was him who had the idea of doing a new album but we had to do it in

August at some point while the studio was free – and this was in late June. We had about four or five songs that had been knocking about for a few years so we needed about eight more. I wrote six songs in a couple of days when Rob was away and we learned them and recorded them in the last two possible days to do it before we wouldn't be allowed in. A very Shrug move… always late, always last minute. We had three full-band rehearsals and that was it. We went in for a day and got all the drums and bass and guitars done, then Rob did all his vocals the next day. Rob also had two spoken word tracks he wanted to do so I put music to them too, then we got it mastered and I did the artwork and it went off to be pressed – written, recorded and out in the space of about four months. It was quite scary to follow up a debut album almost thirty years later but I deffo thought we should do one, although the others took some convincing. I have loved the first Shrug record since I was a kid and still think it's the best album ever made in Middlesbrough."

Arguably, the album's centrepiece, The Apparition, is a spoken word piece inspired by a story told by Robert's good friend, the singer Elaine Palmer.

Rob says, "I've known Elaine since she was a teenager when her band, Aroma, were on before us. We had an hour slot for both of us and they just played for an hour but I thought she was such a talented singer. She told me that one Christmas she saw this ghostly figure walking across her yard at Danby Mill. Her parents knew the guy whose ghost it was, it had been a young boy when he worked there as a miller. Her dad restored the watermill and he'd come back for an open day… I just wondered was it possible that as an old man, he might have seen the apparition of himself. And she said she saw him clearly. The whole house used to creak in all sorts of ways, adjoining a river and old house, rooms that were never opened and freezing cold. Oli wanted to make it a spoken word song."

Elaine says, "Yes, I first met Rob at The Cornerhouse in Middlesbrough. I was in a trio called Aroma and, yes, we totally misjudged our set because we hadn't really played any gigs before and played way over. I think Shrug were on after us so Rob was getting all worked up about his set, ready to go on with his make up and started pacing about, ha! He introduced himself afterwards though and said he thought we were fab!

"I grew up in a very old watermill up on the North Yorkshire moors. My dad still lives there now. It has lots of wonderful and spooky history and features in many publications about the history in the area. There are many millers that have lived and died in the mill and a couple of them still haunt the floors in the mill now. Growing up, every now and then we would hear and even see a dusty flour-coloured figure passing through the courtyard or climbing the old stairs. I told Rob about these tales and he featured them in one of his songs."

The band recorded the album over a couple of weekends but then Nigel wanted to produce each song individually so that took a while, as he had to do that on an evening around his regular job, but Oli went in and helped out with that.

Oli says, "I went back in alone with Nigel and added some extra guitars, a bit of extra drums and some organ, and then one other night I went in with Rob and Nigel and we did the two spoken word tracks in one session. Nigel sent me some rough mixes, I made some notes and he did a final mix and it was off to be mastered by Anthony Chapman. I made the artwork when my boss at my old job wasn't looking… the whole thing from writing it to pressing it took about a month. Making records is easy… haha!"

In fact, one of Oli's other musical endeavours (along with Ajay Saggar), King Champion Sounds, first happened after he and Robert got up on stage with an Austrian dub band Shrug were playing with and improvised with them…

"Ha, I'd forgotten about that," says Oli, "we did a short Dutch tour in 2010 to promote a split 7" we'd done with The Bent Moustache (Ajay's band before King Champion Sounds) and we took this Austrian dub duo called Hey-O-Hansen with us… they were ace. On the last night, we had a massive jam in the venue after we'd all played but it was still open and I ended up playing bass for them for hours. Rob and Ajay got up and did stints too."

Ajay remembers, "That was a tour I arranged for Shrug and Hey-O-Hansen. They played a show at a local venue called De Groote Weiver. At the end of Hey-O Hansen's set they invited Rob to do vocals and Oli to play bass on one track."

"When the idea of King Champion Sounds came up – initially for one show only – Oli was the guy I asked. I guess if I hadn't met him through his involvement with Shrug, then I wouldn't have been able to ask him to join the band."

And that in essence was Shrug part two. Oli appears very much the glue that holds the rest of the band together. For their part, they seem happy to go along with this. A coherence that perhaps would not be there otherwise… like the string on a much-loved package.

12. MIDDLESBROUGH, 2015

It might sound like Robert was living the dream but, although the fanzine was his main income, he always made money elsewhere to help pay the bills. Freelance, if you like, which also sounds overly glamorous in a cut-throat workplace, and, while he always adopted a purist approach to his work and maintains integrity at all costs, this was not without its pitfalls.

He recalls one time, saying, "I was brought in as an outsider by Middlesbrough Council to work as a festival organiser but I was dealing with people who were running galleries and museums or services who weren't allowed to speak to me without going through their manager. I wasn't allowed to speak to anyone directly. I was co-ordinating local history in Middlesbrough. I've done it quite a few times, put lots of events together… getting brochures published and then making sure that it all worked. The then mayor, Ray Mallon, had introduced this culture where you had to speak to a hundred people and there was always somebody else above you and in between."

In 1994 Rob had started writing music pieces for the Teesside Gazette newspaper. His Friday night columns became a go to for local bands hoping to get a helping hand as he waxed lyrically and enthusiastically about anything and everything Teesside. It was an obvious culmination of years of groundwork…

"I was writing for a lot of different people, he says, "lots of different post-punk things, other people's zines, as well as my own. A couple of times, I tried to exist on a government scheme where you would get paid for producing a 'what's on' magazine. Pete Bell did one. I had one called Ket and tried to do that every month. A couple of years later I tried it again with one called One Giant Leap, which was a sister production to Fly Me To The Moon and was mainly music and art in the area, supposedly paid for by a few adverts. Bob Fischer wrote for One Giant Leap as well. We tried to make it quite entertaining and chatty in style. Short sentences and paragraphs, which works well online now. A5 fanzines were always so they could fit in your pocket and the easiest way to break that up on the page was two columns and shorter sentences were easier to read. My mam used to keep all the cuttings long ago. But she's gone now, as have the cuttings. I'm guessing it was about 1994 that I started with the Gazette. It was once a week on a weekend. Friday and then Saturday. I was given a brief to do what I wanted really, writing about live gigs. The then Deputy Editor, Peter Montellier, told me to describe the venue and gig so he could decide if he might fancy going next week. I always kept that in mind and I often wrote for bands' parents, as well as the bands! I tried to provide something they could put in their bios, as well as a review and a nice quote, if possible. Often there was more than one gig featured each week. Towards the end, we had photos as well from Tracy Hyman."

Indeed, when I first moved to the area in 2012, it was my first 'in' to the local music scene. However, an acrimonious split with the Gazette in summer 2016 eventually led Robert to the door of Claire Dupree-Jeans of NARC Magazine, the Newcastle based music and culture freesheet, and, as we would expect by now, something of a convoluted turn of events.

Tracy says, "I first met Rob at Tees Music Alliance in Stockton. At the time The Green Room wasn't a venue with a stage, it had a little kitchen area in the back left corner and a DIY gallery space on the wall opposite. I volunteered with Tees Music Alliance, at the time featuring bands like Pellethead and members of Dressed Like Wolves and other eclectic characters, with pay what you like tea and coffees and microwave cakes. I remember standing behind the counter and making the drinks and chatting to people, and amongst those who put in a regular appearance was Rob. This was about 2009. He was often reviewing gigs for the Gazette and generally supporting the local music scene. From then on we became friends. I started taking photos for NARC and just generally photographing gigs around The Georgian Theatre a lot."

Rob adds, "I wrote the column for the Gazette for years, about four hundred words a week but it often got chopped to pieces depending what else was on the page. I fancied it being a column so I put stuff to do with myself in to personalise it. I got a bit annoyed with the way they were editing it so I'd start with a line and then finish with a corresponding line because they were just chopping the end off, so at least then they would have to think about how they were editing it. The stuff I reviewed I never asked for tickets or guestlists from the Gazette and in the end that came back to bite me. I'd arranged my own access with the venues and I did that for years and then we fell out because for Deer Shed Festival that year they had given the tickets to somebody else and I was furious because I'd set it up and I'd been setting it up for years on behalf of the Gazette. I started getting a bit annoyed when they started giving the sports guy Cattle & Cane reviews. I didn't even get a fee at first but then I got £25, then £40 but then it ended because Trinity Mirror said they were stopping all freelance work nationally. Then Peter [Montellier] went back in as stand-in editor and I said I'd come back in again with Tracy, and she would do photos, if he could look at some way of remunerating us. He said he would look at using an advert to pay for us, but then he didn't get the job."

Tracy remembers, "At some point the editor changed and discussions were made about continuing the column, On The Beat. We started reviewing any local gig we fancied, or thought should gain public attention, once a week. Sometimes reviewing more than one gig a week, or even more than one on the same night. We had some quite magical experiences and discoveries through On The Beat. I remember one stormy night with flooded roads… a night with at least three gigs on across Teesside, where we decided to go to The Georgian Theatre to see Cerys Matthews, the backdrop was a fireplace on the screen behind and it was just lovely and cosy and intimate. How did the column end? The feeling that it perhaps wasn't valued as much as it should be. A comment about how we needed to go through the paper to get entry to gigs and festivals so we wouldn't tread on other reporters' toes, when we had been arranging entry with the promoters, bands and event organisers ourselves for years. Which is what we had to do, or most of the reviews wouldn't have happened, I suppose."

In fact, a campaign on The Northern Line website, which celebrates 'irreverent northern culture', sought to save Robert's On The Beat feature in 2010. Alas, as of 2021, there were no comments on the site.

As time goes on, it starts to look like a bad luck story. Robert was part of the Love Middlesbrough project before the council co-opted the website name for their own magazine, and he wrote blogs on there for a number of years before falling out with them because he was getting paid such a small amount of money and then suddenly got a memo saying he wasn't allowed to mention anything outside of Middlesbrough Council jurisdiction.

"I was only mentioning Stockton and Redcar stuff," he says, "so it was still Teesside. So, on all sorts of levels, the councils weren't talking to each other even back then. Yaffa Phillips and Claire Wordsworth left their roles at Middlesbrough Council so the new marketing people changed the whole way of doing it, but they had the thing where I could only write about Middlesbrough so I couldn't even write about a Middlesbrough band playing in Stockton. It was so parochial. I was really lucky with Claire and Yaffa, who were the driving force behind Love Middlesbrough, and they were great innovators. They came up with an approach for me to write for the blog, which was tremendous. I did get hampered for a time but we moved on from that and I was so lucky to be able to blog about the town and its people for five years. Basically, Claire left and Yaffa changed jobs, then Love Middlesbrough changed direction. Yaffa passed away a couple of years ago and is so missed by everyone. She was a massive supporter of local gigs and bands, cafés, museums, everything Middlesbrough, and, coming from New York, brought an international perspective to everything. She has left an unfillable hole."

If there is a trend here regarding money and freelancing, it will be something that any writer will be familiar with. In a serious journalistic environment, a freelancer can easily find themselves spending as much time chasing up small invoices from unscrupulous editors or, worse still, invoicing publications who have used work without permission, than the writing itself. Add to that lead-in times that often mean real hourly rates work out way below minimum wage – and workflow is either on or off – meaning a regular forty-hour week is a luxury most cannot afford. These lead-in times on major articles or getting a regular gig with an established publication mean freelancing remains, to most, a labour of love.

Robert was already well versed in this environment, having previously written for a glossy magazine that came out of Newcastle called Paint It Red, and had done so for quite a while before Fly Me To The Moon, which gave him a good grounding for the Gazette column.

"The Gazette column really did help the music scene," he says, "the people putting on the gigs really appreciated it and the fans used to come up and tell me I was always positive… the music scene needed all the help it could get at the time. There was no radio play or anything for them at that time. I started writing for NARC when the Gazette thing finished but I really only do albums. The hundred and twenty word limit is quite a skill. Claire [Dupree-Jeans, editor] was coming to do something at the Town Hall. My friend, Jamie Sample, kept telling me NARC was doing something in Teesside and Claire came and talked about expanding the magazine's reach into the area and she asked me to send her some stuff. There was a gap with the Gazette and then I went back unpaid for a bit around the same time. I've only ever just written bits for NARC though. I've not done many interviews. I did interview Mark E Smith for NARC… I think everyone else was a bit afraid. I had a mutual friend and, as an opening line, I mentioned him and we were away. It was amazing to interview someone I had been listening to and following since I was a teenager."

Claire says, "I think it was after a Q&A event NARC and Generator NE did with Maximo Park in Middlesbrough but I can't be a hundred per cent certain. I know when Rob comes to me with an idea or volunteers to write something that he's already invested and passionate about his subject matter. He's the sort of writer whose passion is evident from the moment he puts pen to paper; you can almost see the way his brain is working at a hundred miles an hour in his stream of consciousness-style reviewing, desperate to get the words out and his points made. He makes it his business to know about his subject, and that really comes across in his writing. Every time we meet he tells me something new about a project he's working on – often based in the local community – and if there's something worth knowing about the area, I can guarantee that Rob knows about it first."

To those unfamiliar with Robert's writing style, he is clever and witty but, most of all, inclusive in his approach… that holy trinity of simplicity, indulgence and flair that keeps both avid readers and cursory browsers interested. While Fly Me To The Moon has evolved over the years, it has always managed to retain a style that appeals to young and old alike, and true to Rob's assertions that it has to appeal to all demographics (and the main reason there is rarely any swearing in the magazine).

For the Gazette music column, in all its guises over the years, and more latterly NARC Magazine, Robert has allowed his more creative urges to flow in a series of cleverly crafted and knowledgeable pieces.

His contributions to Love Middlesbrough website, Local History Month and the various other endeavours over the years, as we have seen, mean he can easily turn his writing hand to anything these days… a rare gift indeed.

Robert also wrote a number of Fly Me To The Moon

football columns for the Hartlepool Mail in late 2020. These were a continuation of his inimitable style, in one joshing with manager Neil Warnock about getting away to Darlington during the traditional winter break in lockdown, but perhaps more of an indicator as to how Rob intends to extend the Fly Me To The Moon brand in the coming years.

Elsewhere in his media ventures, Robert has immersed himself in some occasionally absurd antics on the radio. Usually with his good friend Bob Fischer.

"Over the years I've done quite a lot on BBC Tees," Rob says. "It was John Foster who asked if I'd like to come in to preview the gigs, then, when he was away, Bob would do the show and I started sitting in, for like an hour, and fill the program just chatting to each other. That's so hard, just being able to talk to yourself on the radio. Bob got into that through a few of us going to away matches. Clem always wanted to be the marketing officer for the club and they put an idea together for an alternative radio programme… a bit like taking the fanzine onto the radio like Baddiel and Skinner who were taking fanzine ideas onto TV. They called it Red Balls of Fire, packaged it up and sent it to so many radio stations. BBC Tees were the only ones who got back to them. Fischer honed his skills and Clem went off and did national TV, Grandstand, 5 Live and stuff like that. We've been friends since the 80s, but I've been doing the show with Fischer on a Thursday night for a few years."

More recently Rob has done some music previews for

the show and based on that, he now thinks the music scene in the region has never been so strong, both in terms of quality and quantity.

"There are so many great bands," he says. "So many great, dedicated promoters, brilliant music press and radio and most of all such a great audience. Or audiences, because you need lots of different people for a music scene to thrive. It will die with what could become a clique."

Which all sounds like great fun but broadcasting is a serious business and to be able to bring one of his passions onto a BBC platform is an achievement in itself. But, arguably the pinnacle of Robert's philanthropic efforts was when he got the Mayor's Award from Ray Mallon in 2015.

"Oh yes," he says, "that was quite a surprise and obviously a real honour. I got to invite friends and family to the mayor's parlour. I felt it was very special because it was all about service to Middlesbrough where I have lived and worked nearly all the years since I was born. There is Fly Me To The Moon, the fanzine and the message board community, speaking up for Middlesbrough and along with Tracy Hyman organising annual events with Discover Middlesbrough and Local History Month which we did for several years – all about bringing together local volunteers and community groups as well as museums, archives and galleries and pulling together programmes that hopefully entertain and promote all the different things to do and see in Middlesbrough."

As a postscript of sorts, and to take this part of Rob's story back to its beginnings, in December 2020 Robert released a book of his own, entitled My Boro Debut, which is a collection of fans and former players reminiscing about their first visits to Ayresome Park or the Riverside, which presented a rare opportunity for fans and players alike to recall a similar and shared, if physically and temporally separate experience, and a canny way of taking a step back, as the pandemic has afforded many of us, to take stock and reflect...

Rob says, "I would probably like to follow that up with another publication based on peoples' memories. And I'm thinking about whether there might be spin offs from the fanzine in book form. One of the long running columns is really funny and surreal and we might try and edit a collection together as a book."

Rob contacted me, well into the editing process of this book, and told me about another project he had been asked to get involved with.

"I had to take a day out today to be filmed walking around Ayresome Park," he told me, "for some film makers from London wanting to explore community in red wall towns... but not in a patronising way. Their films will be called Northern Exposure and they filmed some asylum seekers working in allotments in Albert Park. I had no idea those allotments were even present, did you?" And, "Oh, I need to write some music as well, don't I?!" was all Robert would say alluding to the possibility of a third Shrug album.

Throughout our get-togethers and correspondence, I got the feeling that it was often the writing itself that was driving Robert as much as the football and the music. It's clear that, along with his broader media work, it's another genuine passion of his as it became increasingly difficult, at times, to unknot (that string metaphor again) the multiple facets of his creative endeavours. It would be surprising, in that respect, if Robert does not take more of a media-based path in the future, even after Fly Me To The Moon has been passed to the next generation of supporters. Something his tentative steps into book publishing might signal as a potentially new and exciting development in the life of someone who knows, arguably, more about his chosen subjects than anyone else in the area.

13. TOFT HOUSE, 2020

So, if Shrug in the late 1980s and 90s were formidable, Shrug today are no less of a force, even if they are now limiting themselves to three or four carefully selected shows per year. At a near sold out Toft House in Middlesbrough in January 2020, breaking the attendance record for the venue and the first show of the band's fifth decade together, Robert still managed to fit in an impressive amount of costume changes (three horse head masks in one song, no less, as well as his traditional Captain Cook outfit). If Oli appears to hold it all together musically that is only because the rest of the band are still busy having as much fun as they possibly can. On the drums, Richie is unassuming and tight (though with a razor wit between songs when the mood takes him), Kev on bass is steady as a rock and Richard on guitar spends most of the time with his back to the audience, seemingly intent only on watching the rest of the band as they are so good. Only Sarah is missing on this occasion. Life does get in the way sometimes.

Michael Baines from support act on the night, Werbeniuk, remembers that gig affectionately. "The Toft House gig was only the second time that Shrug and Werbeniuk had played on the same bill. The first being a few months earlier at the Studio 64 reunion at Doc Brown's, but the Toft House gig seemed more special. It was the last gig I played or attended before the pandemic. It was one of those gigs where there was much catching up and 'I've not seen you in twenty years!' being spoken between folk."

Despite the glacially slow album cycles, Shrug released a surprising amount of singles and EPs back in the day.

"Rough Trade did one with us," Rob says. "We played with another of Ian Armstrong's Meantime signings, Wat Tyler, and the drummer Sean worked for Rough Trade. He said he could press a single really cheap when Dale was the guitarist with us in the mid-90s."

Beardo Weirdo was released on Sean's Rugger Bugger Discs imprint in 1992 and is perhaps Shrug's best-known track…

However, exacerbated by the band's dislike of the CD format and early social media such as MySpace, as well as the fact that people didn't want to buy records anymore, the band stopped releasing official singles.

"I'm still rubbish at digital and downloads," says Rob. "When I review stuff for NARC, I always lose the links so I haven't even got any of those albums I've reviewed."

Oli has since put everything on Bandcamp, so the band's official back catalogue is well documented although Robert confesses the band still played many songs for which they don't remember the music or lyrics that are lost forever.

"It just doesn't exist anymore, I suppose," he admits.

Oli says of Bandcamp, "Yeah, that took a long time to

do! It needed doing though, and no one else seemed to want to do it so I did it… mainly to save more stuff from being lost. Plus, I like things to be organised so it's nice to have everything in one place. I think I did it around 2010? A total chore but it was nice to hear stuff I'd never heard before."

Then, around the same time, after twenty five years together the band were asked by then council Arts & Events Co-ordinator Nicky Peacock to open a pop-up shop on Linthorpe Road for a week where they decked out the whole shop with photos and letters.

"I had this file of letters," Rob says, "that we put up on the wall People had written to us as teenagers, sometimes people would write with problems and we used to do lots with fanzines and be on compilation tapes, loads around the country. We had a room at the back with loads of videos of TV stuff on a loop."

Talking to Rob, you get the feeling it is sometimes only when he gets this sort of chance to take stock and coalesce memories and long forgotten episodes that he really gets the chance to set out the Shrug story for the remarkable one that it is, although he remains almost steadfastly prosaic in his recollections.

He says, "We did some sort of parade and bands went round on trucks, only they had forgotten to put petrol in the generator so we basically just drove around playing drums and bits of metal [to make as much noise as possible]. I don't know what year it was."

Drummer Michael Sanderson says, "Yeah, that was on

a Saturday. 30th April 1988, to be precise. A May Day rally. Some of the photos were on the insert that came with the Nevil Wanless EP. The rally started on the roadside of Albert Park and went out onto Linthorpe Road, Corporation Road and through town when the road used to run through from the bus station to the Town Hall but the generator ran out before we got there. The set list was Van With Square Wheels, Joe 90, Sir Walter Raleigh, Living On An Aeroplane, Archie Stephens, Camel In Ice, Joe 90 (again), Yankee From Gdansk. It all lasted about thirty minutes."

Middlesbrough Music Collective also used to hold an annual festival in the quadrangle of the Town Hall so, naturally Shrug played, and there followed another festival called Lark in the Park in 1995, near the Bottle of Notes, which preceded Middlesbrough Music Live.

"Probably where they got the idea from," Rob says. "I had the idea of it being Captain Cook themed so we got a dinghy and I dressed as Cook. The band that were meant to be on before us got lost in town – because they wanted to play later – so we suddenly had to go on an hour earlier and we hadn't blown the boat up. I was sinking so Bob Fischer had to pull it across and nobody knew what was going on…"

Bob elaborates on the tale. "I remember it being a beautiful sunny day. Robert was dressed as Captain Cook, and decided it might be fun to arrive onstage in a nautical fashion, sailing across an uncharted ocean (the little lake behind the stage) then leaping from his mighty vessel (a tiny dinghy) before launching straight into the opening song…

"I was pressganged into being his 'crew'. I was wearing a fisherman's hat and a jaunty neckerchief, and the pair of us were shoved into the decidedly wobbly-looking dinghy as the rest of the band began to play the opening bars on the main stage. It became apparent at this point that one oar was twice as long as the other. With the dinghy shoved into the centre of the lake by a few forceful boots from the audience, I tried to paddle furiously, but we only succeeded in going around in circles.

"Onstage, the rest of the band continued to play the opening bars of the first song. Over and over. In my head, it went on for about twenty minutes, while we shouted for help. Eventually some bright spark found a rope, which was thrown to us from the shore, and we were hauled to safety. Robert (costume now slightly soggy) leapt onto the stage as though the whole routine had been meticulously planned! Then, at the end of the show, our friend Stuart Downing chased Robert to the Bottle of Notes before theatrically beating him to death while shouting 'Aloha from Hawaii, Captain Cook!'"

Another time, the band roped in keyboardist Sarah's then five-year-old daughter Melanie to sing joint lead vocals. Ironically she was a future classmate of Oli, as Robert recalls. "She performed at a school fete at Abingdon Road School… there was a gig festival. I think she also played at one of the Middlesbrough Music Live gigs in the Town Hall courtyard. Melanie would be clutching an animal toy as she was singing… probably Sir Walter Raleigh's Fast Food Take Over – where she could shout out 'desperate for chips and blue trousers' – about the perils of sitting on a park bench that had just been painted. Get them in while they are young!"

The visual accoutrements had become more and more absurd as time went on and they often went wrong in slapstick Some Mothers Do 'Ave 'Em fashion.

"I remember in Holland once," Rob says, "I saw a shopping trolley, so I got dressed up in lots of different gear with a dinosaur head and got someone to pull this trolley towards the stage, but I hadn't noticed there was a lip. So, that was the start of the gig, the shopping trolley went flying and I just fell out on the floor.

"There was a band called HTQ where the singer used to run onstage and tag the backwall, and [The Ex frontman] GW Sok used to run on the spot, so I combined the two. When we toured with The Ex, I'd jump off stage and run around the crowd, but they were big venues with high stages and, as I jumped to get back on stage, I hit the corner and split my leg open and had to have it bandaged for the rest of the tour.

"The idea with punk and post-punk bands was that you had just come off the street but we wanted to make it always like a performance because it wasn't complicated music so we'd find ways to make things intense and engaging. One of the first gigs I ever saw at the Rock Garden on Newport Road in March 1979 was The Skids and they only had half a dozen songs that they just played again and again and they kept saying, 'We only know three chords… you can do this'."

For Middlesbrough Music Collective, this kind of grassroots DIY thinking was a lifeblood – and to some extent continues to this day – as they strove to develop a viable scene and secure enough funding to at least break even. Robert's sense of community spirit is to be admired, especially as he has matured. When, for many, that socialist spark wanes, Robert's never has. Still a stalwart of the local gig community to this day, his ideals spill over into all aspects of his life. Life, after all, is a shared experience and for Rob that has meant never selling out and retaining the straight-off-the-street punk spirit… but, for many, as something they are passionate about gets more successful, it naturally becomes more of a business enterprise…

"When we got Studio 64," he says, "because that was a really big thing to get a community recording studio, there was a focus then on getting a venue. Red Wedge came to Middlesbrough with John Prescott, and Shrug auditioned to support Billy Bragg at Thornaby Pavilion, and the conclusion from that was that they could use sports centres. That fizzled out but shortly after the Arena started in the old Rock Garden venue with Graham Ramsey from Ten Feet Tall. With that the need for a venue dissipated, the collective started fragmenting as that collectivised era had run its course.

"The fanzine had already started but I was just writing for it and that's how I'd been able to get involved…

through the collective and other music writing. Julia Burgess took over as gig secretary and took the gigs to the downstairs back room in The Empire but it wasn't really a collective anymore. I put on bands like The Membranes, Snuff, No Means No, The Ex with their fire engine from Netherlands, Thrilled Skinny from Luton, Dandelion Adventure (Ajay's band), as well as lots of local bands like Spit the Pips, Icy Eye… it was all a collective effort."

The council had helped…

He adds, "Before I got involved they had helped get a portable studio, a four-track, which was great, all analogue gear. They supported stuff as venues came and went. It was better than the 70s. When I was growing up and going to gigs, everything was dark and grey. There is loads of nostalgia for that era but it was really aggressive and violent…"

That same underdog spirit still lives on, particularly in the Whirling Dervish night which continues on a weekly basis on Thursday nights at Sticky Fingers on Linthorpe Road, having gone through a number of incarnations and venues including the Princess Alice and TS One, and has hosted everyone and anyone from the local music scene of recent years including Mouses, Be Quiet. Shout Loud! and Dylan Cartlidge. Places like Base Camp in Exchange Square very much stick to a DIY blueprint with an open-door policy on promoters and acts, while changes to licensing laws in recent years have meant anywhere from art galleries, empty shops, restaurants and even derelict old houses can put on live music.

I asked Robert if he was happy with the Shrug's recorded output.

"The Neville Wanless EP, even though it was only 8 track, you can hear that it was really well produced being on 12" with the big grooves. The first album didn't really sound as bright, which was a shame, but it was still good, but then the last album we got two mixes done, one for digital and one for vinyl. That was producer Anthony Chapman's idea. I've often got a different ear to it than Oli. I would produce the drums better on many tracks but he might not agree."

Apropos to nothing, Robert says, "I interviewed Mark E Smith once about a Fall album called Ersatz, and he said how he kept listening to it and eventually decided he couldn't listen again and just said yes to the mix."

With the band's popularity in Europe, it's perhaps surprising there haven't been more EPs and albums, but it seems logistics always got in the way. I did wonder whether Robert preferred touring Europe to the UK?

He explains, "There was always a big difference between playing in Britain and in Europe. We played with The Ex at the Paradiso in Amsterdam – the night after the Velvet Underground had played the same venue – then we came back to London to play a gig at which not even the promoter turned up... there was only my brother and his girlfriend there. In Europe, you got well looked after... food, accommodation and a dressing room. In Holland, there were government subsidies paid to the venues and they monitored attendances year by year, week on week… it was part of their culture. In Middlesbrough, The Kids Are Solid Gold and Steve Harland do the same thing… looking after the bands before and after, but for a long time it was terrible. We played a gig in Ipswich and, after we played, the promoter wanted me to pay them thirty quid to let our van out. That sort of thing puts you off. We did a lot of gigs with Luton's Thrilled Skinny, who I'm still friends with now. We played a couple of gigs in Bedford and Peterborough and there were some really bad fights in the audience. We played at The Square in Harlow and it was a fantastic enthusiastic crowd, including Anthony Chapman, and, being local authority, they could pay you a proper fee and tour promoters could use the gig to subsidise the gigs in London where acts often got totally ripped off."

And, I had to ask Robert what his parents made of it all.

"They came to see us a couple of times," he says. "We played once in Coulby Newham in the Parkway Centre in a shop and it was terrible. They were music fans, but not punk fans. They went along with it and, because my vans were second hand and kept clapping out or getting smashed up or whatever, they helped me buy a new van and kit it out and make sure it was safe. So, they did help me but that was the van that crashed!"

Robert has had two write-offs. The second was on a New Year's Eve in the middle of Middlesbrough when an unofficial taxi went straight through a red light and spun the van around. He wasn't hurt but the insurers wrote it off.

"We sometimes play in Newcastle," he says, "and a really nice theatre venue in North Shields and a lass put on a couple of gigs in Leeds because she really liked our music but we really only play outside of Teesside on request now. I did play a couple on my own in Leeds in 2018. That was nerve-wracking. I didn't understand the technology so I asked Leddie MC what to do. I did it all on my phone but it kept going off!"

Leddie says, "I told him I use an iPod and he asked if it's possible to do the same on his phone. I said just create a playlist and let your set run through so you can be free on stage and know what's next. As long as his phone is on silent... He told me he had managed to edit his tracks and put them on his phone and had run through it a few times successfully. I'm also bad with technology and was completely nervous for him in case I messed up his gig!"

As football took priority over the band, I wondered how the rest of the band took that.

"[They] probably got really annoyed," Robert states tacitly.

Did they ever fall out?

"All the time," he says. "We got offered a gig in Holland at Christmas-time… for quite a bit of money, a football/music gig, but it was during the football season, so…

"Chumbawamba became famous, and we knew people like that. We could support them and people would really enjoy us and we could hold our own with all of those bands, so I was terrible really because we could have done a lot more…"

However, when I ask Robert of his one overriding memory of the band, I'm not surprised by his response.

"Going to East Berlin," he says. "I still think back, and to have been there as it was happening. It will forever be an important part of European history.

"It was exciting times and we became a part of a sort of scene if you like, people like Thrilled Skinny, Membranes, Dandelion Adventure, Death by Milkfloat, No Means No, Blyth Power, The Fflaps, Snuff, The Pralines, Dog Faced Hermans, and Buy Off The Bar. To this day, we are still friends with many of these people. Isn't that amazing? Sometimes you don't hear from someone for years. Just last week I became friends with Joseph Porter of Blyth Power on Facebook after a break of over twenty years.

"But also, we've put some music out on the planet that people have enjoyed and smiled at." Then, as if on cue, Robert remembers a little anecdote to square this circle quite nicely. "We played at Doctor Brown's for the Studio 64 revival gig in 2019," when Carl drummed for the first time in years, "and the band were packing up so I just did a song on my own… called No Ball Games from the first EP and this girl came up and asked what it was. She thought it was a cover version because she had been to a gig in Northampton years ago, heard the song, and had sang it all the way home. She told me it was at Northampton Roadmenders… I told her that it was us playing and that it was our own song. That was thirty years before when she was a young girl and she had remembered it all that time. I also went back to Berlin about five years ago when Hey-O-Hansen asked me to go over again and do one song with them but I ended up doing the whole gig. It was fantastic to go back and go on the tour and be able to say to the tour guide at Checkpoint Charlie that I was there when I was. The wall wasn't straight so it's hard to see any join now but we went near where Knaack had been, and the venue we played with Hey-O-Hansen would have been in East Germany too."

And of course, I wanted to know if Robert had brought a historic souvenir back from that first trip to Berlin.

"I brought some pieces of the wall back," he says, "but I lost it all. They were just chippings. My mam washed me coat… she said the pockets were full of dust!"

14. LINTHORPE VILLAGE, 2021

While it may now seem like a long time since the infamous locking of the gates in 1986, Linthorpe Village today is still a hub of working class activity, a cultural melting pot of languages and heritage, young couples buying their first homes and pensioners who've been there all their lives. While the exploding student population has yet to reach this part of town, there is no doubt it is still an integral part of Middlesbrough's present and future. And while Ayresome Park itself may be long gone, the sympathetic redevelopment of the site means, amongst the traditional back-to-back terraces, the newer houses there are a permanent reminder of the past and a striking juxtaposition even at twenty years old themselves. And one that means, to a keen eye, or particularly from the air, it is still easy to pick out the outline of the old ground. While on the pitch, it might often seem like the blink of an eye as managers and players have come and gone, not to mention a series of cup runs, a trophy and the odd controversial relegation, nobody would have dared predict the transition of the club from old third division to Wembley, to a UEFA Cup final and most of the way back again, within a third of a century of nearly going out of business for good.

Of the club's recent managers, Robert is unapologetically honest about Jonathan Woodgate being given a fair crack of the managerial whip, crucially seeing some similarities between him and England manager Gareth Southgate. "I was always behind him but people have low tolerances. Pulis is a prisoner of his past because he's known to play terrible football but I'm not sure if he does really… people just don't enjoy it. All the fans have preconceptions about managers, they certainly don't think people can change. He was a decent bloke Pulis. You won't get many fans reminiscing about Southgate either. They still see him as the rookie manager. They don't take on board that somebody grows and learns, especially someone like Southgate, because we got relegated, but he's a man that studies things. And so is Woodgate."

While the Warnock era was predictably divisive, the club's fans seem more content with a more experienced manager in charge and his often unorthodox approach was refreshing to many after a period of treading football water and, having extended his initial short-term contract, it appeared the appreciation was mutual. The journeyman manager injected a much needed enthusiasm into the squad, while his penchant for flowing football and giving young players a chance galvanised the supporters once more. The more recent appointment of Chris Wilder to the manager's role is at least an extension of this ethos as he will bring a similar no-nonsense approach to managing the team while also not being afraid to be innovative with tactics and formations that should similarly endear him to many fans.

Of previous managers, Rob is refreshingly forthright despite his protestations of broad positivity. Of Karanka he says, "He was very controlling. He had a strange personality, I think. He was very, very friendly and very warm but then very controlling about lots of things. He insisted on being the chief coach and not the manager. He almost didn't want to sign the players and let someone else take responsibility then slag them off. He was an odd man. He wouldn't even allow penalties at half-time on the pitch because of the damage to the pitch. Sadly he had to go, and, with hindsight, the decision was made too late to save our season and Premier League status. Karanka was targeting fourth bottom and getting to survival almost incrementally through draws. When teams like Crystal Palace, Leicester and Swansea revived, we did not, or could not, respond and change our tactics."

On another former manager with an international pedigree, Rob tells me, "Steve McClaren was a fantastic cup manager. Again, people used to say he was a lucky manager, as if you would want an unlucky manager! A lot of managers are judged on what they say after a match and he was thinking about what he was saying and what his players would think and what messages they would get from it."

•

Two Unsung Heroes… while it's all this camaraderie that shines like a beacon in much of Robert's story, it's important to return again to the selfless aspect of Robert's infectious personality. Again, almost as an afterthought,

Robert sent me a message on Facebook to tell me about his good friend Bjarte from Bergen in Norway, who has a season ticket next to Robert at the Riverside even though he can only afford to come over several times a season,

Rob says, "I get tickets for him and a lot of other Norwegian fans who travel over to watch Boro games, but also groundhopping, travelling around the country ticking off grounds and making friends. Each year they raise hundreds of pounds to help local supporters get to matches they couldn't afford otherwise."

And, Yvonne Ferguson is the fans liaison officer at the club who makes sure every penny Bjarte raises (over £1,000 in the last two seasons) goes to a good cause. Yvonne will also contact Robert if she hears about a fan that has died and then reaches out to the family to see if she can help in some way.

Rob says of the pair's work, "Nobody else really knows about these little gestures but it could just be getting the family a chance to sit in their relative's seat or just to chat at the club."

Bjarte says, "SK Brann appointed Bill Elliot as coach in 1973 and he managed to get many English football clubs to play and I think the first one was Middlesbrough FC in April 1974. I didn't have a favourite English team at that time, so when Middlesbrough came to Brann Stadium I went to the game with a notebook for autographs. I went early and got all the players – and Jackie Charlton's – and from that day I was addicted to Middlesbrough FC as my English football club. I love Middlesbrough FC and I love

Middlesbrough as a town, so I and the others just want to give something back. We have always been treated very well and we all know different people in Middlesbrough, so it is our way to say thank you to both club and town. The people of Bergen are known as very patriotic and we say we are not from Norway, we're from Bergen. And we love our history. And for me it is what Rob does for Middlesbrough. He is a huge Middlesbrough FC fan, but also very interested of the history of Middlesbrough, Teesside and the North East. His interest in culture and art is so enormous and genuine, he is a really good man for Middlesbrough that I'm very proud of having as a really good friend."

Yvonne adds, "I've been at the club twenty five years but seven seasons ago I helped set up the Family Zone. We invite families for every home game and special event throughout the year. We also invite care homes, veterans and homeless people with reallocated tickets that supporters have donated. I didn't know Bjarte but Rob introduced us and when I took him to see the Family Zone, he was blown away and from then on he started doing some fundraising every season. Middlesbrough is a club that is very passionate about our supporters and I often ask Rob to pass on my details to supporters who make comments on FMTTM. Rob is very proactive and we work very closely as the club is a focal point of the community. He's quite shy naturally but when he's in his comfort zone he is very passionate, he's such a nice guy."

Rob has not missed a single match home or away since his brother Stephen's wedding in Hong Kong in 1999, even then only going over for three days so as not to miss the following game. It has become something of an obsession for him.

He says, "I'd missed a match the season before when Graham Ramsay got married in New York but that was just a League Cup game and then…"

I wondered out loud, as it seemed incredible his own brother had not checked the fixture list.

"It was ridiculous," he says, "but I only missed one match. I'm usually at around seventy of the league grounds but it goes up and down. I sometimes think about going to the others in between Boro games but I'm not that ridiculous! People like Bjarte are proper groundhoppers… he and his late brother Kjell actually completed all our ninety two league grounds years ago."

However, Robert does occasionally go to other games and in 2010 he took a trip to South Africa with his good friend Geoff Vickers, who organised the whole thing.

"It was an amazing experience," he says. "World Cups and European Championships always are. The countries and, in this case, the continent want to show themselves to you in the best possible light, and show off their culture to make it an unforgettable experience. And it certainly was. We stayed in two different locations in Cape Town, just beneath Table Mountain. We talked to Australian fans about Boro's Australian keeper Mark Schwarzer after we had seen them defeated three-nil by Germany.

We were also invited by Paul Armstrong to the Match of the Day studio in Cape Town before we travelled to Durban on an internal airliner… the plane was painted like a cartoon plane and the pilots and stewardesses made jokes throughout the flight… which was surreal. A big positive image for me was the black and white South Africans being very much unified as African, but we also saw the poverty of the shanty towns and people walking along rural roads looking for work or lifts to work. So, you realised you were in the country with perhaps the most revered man alive in Nelson Mandela, who was then still alive… retired but enormously loved and respected. It was an amazing trip, a feast and a festival of football but so, so much more. Of course, we always seem to bump into people we know and, in a bar in Cape Town, we met Viv Anderson, who was assistant manager to Bryan Robson. To see Table Mountain and the Cape of Good Hope, as well as Robben Island, and experience it with people from all around the world coming together… that is the power of football."

•

As an adopted Teessider myself, it is difficult not to feel the impact and passion for Middlesbrough Football Club wherever you turn. Whether that is Middlesbrough being a one-club town, or the working-class roots of a town that had only formed itself fifty years before the football club came into existence, or with the new ground being built in the heart of the industrial old town. Indeed, take a walk from the famous Good Food Joint at the end of Albert Road, past Cineworld, through the subways and over the level crossing with its orderly redbrick signal box, towards the still impressive looking stadium on match days and the natural bonhomie of the fans is infectious. There is an old-fashioned sense of strength in numbers unique to football, particularly when the crowd thickens past Middlesbrough College as the old gates comes into sight in the West Stand car park… a Mackenzie Thorpe waiting to be painted.

15. MIDDLESBROUGH, PRESENT DAY

Under Cleveland's hills, in the constantly imposing distance, pre-historic sediments continue to stratify, perhaps for our ancestors to discover in hundreds, nay thousands, of years from now, long after the last remaining vestiges of industry have crumbled and disappeared back into the earth. Occasional ingots of iron to be belched forth and picked up by future generations and considered quizzically like present day fossils. But, today, a couple of miles away as the crow flies, at Teesaurus dinosaur park, just a few hundred yards along the River Tees from the Transporter Bridge, a lick of paint has given the whole area a welcome lift, bringing the dinosaurs back to life, or at least breathing new air into an area of economic fossilisation. And, as the football transfer window came to a close this year, a flurry of activity at the Riverside Stadium injected a much needed optimism. So, while the floodlights might not be welcoming Europe's football elite again anytime soon, there was a strangely familiar positivity in the air as a full moon shone brightly over Middlehaven.

Pre-Covid, Rob had told me that he had no idea whether he'd still be doing Fly Me To The Moon the following season (2020/21).

"I always make that decision in the summer," he says. "It's quite hard to see how we can do it if we don't stay up. If we could sell it to more people abroad as an email or pdf then that would really help. People have suggested bundling with the website so I might have to look at that as well."

As things panned out over the next few months, the season was suspended and then finished behind closed doors at a rush, and Rob did indeed fulfil his subscriptions with digital bundles. It made sense to continue this into the following campaign, which also started behind closed doors after only the briefest of close seasons.

An interesting footnote to this particular saga, though, is the Middlesbrough game against Bournemouth on 10th October 2020 that was allowed to go ahead in front of 1,000 lucky fans in a trial of socially distanced games. A surreal but memorable experience as Rob explains, "It was a strange experience going back but actually much more successful and uplifting than we might have expected. The few lucky fans did actually build an atmosphere and you could tell from the applause, even for the players warming up, that everyone was just so appreciative of being there. It was all organised so safely, the players and staff appreciated our return and we especially did. After all those years of not missing a match, I was very grateful to be back."

During this time, Robert had also gazumped me by conceptualising, financing and getting published his own book of Boro memories.

"My Boro Debut was the eventual title," he says. "One of the contributors, Gary Bolton, thought that one up. His dad Jack starts the book, taking us back to post WWII and hopefully that gives a bit of a boost to everyone in lockdown year because Jack Bolton takes us back to where everyone filled the stadium, desperate for normality after war. His son, Gary, finishes, taking up the baton from his dad and passing it on to his kids. I think that tells the story of the Boro fan community and how the football club is so important and central to being in or from Teesside. I have had the idea for years but lockdown made me finally go for it – everyone goes to a first match but, unlike first day at school, the timing can be unique, and it's usually the starting point of a lifelong support. So, I thought I'd do it fanzine style and let the fans actually give their own stories in their own words. We can all relate to what they're saying and yet, pulled together, it is a complete cross section of generations over many decades. When we return to the Riverside if people look around them it could be the stories of all those sitting around them."

When I asked Robert what he would do if Fly Me To The Moon was no more, he was typically upbeat for someone who has presided over something so important to many for so long… something that will undoubtedly go down in local lore when that day comes.

"I'd have to retire or get a regular job, I suppose," he says. "But I've saved. I'm alright."

EPILOGUE

Football is and has always been the constant in Rob's life from a young age. Early on in this project, I asked which took precedent, football or music, and straight away he said it was football, with a surprising honesty I would come to admire in him.

In November 2019, Fly Me To The Moon celebrated its 600th edition and I had that in mind when I was forming the idea for this book but it's clear Robert has no intention of relinquishing the responsibility to anyone else... global pandemic and a relegation scrap behind closed doors or not.

The fanzine continues to pay for itself through its advertising and subscriptions, and Robert's public profile means it's an early retirement policy, if not a metaphorical gold watch.

In fact, on each occasion we met up throughout this project, there wasn't one time where at least one person didn't come up and introduce themselves to Robert. I ask if this happens all the time and he laughs a little bashfully and just says, "It's better when we're winning."

And that is Robert in a neat little anecdote. Relaxed, approachable and so easy to be around. While I conceived this book as one about music and football, it became apparent to me that in Robert's life nothing is more important than the people that surround him, so, while this book may have been about football and music, it is really a book about you and me. I suppose.

SHRUG DISCOGRAPHY

ALBUMS

Septober Octember No'Wonder
Meantime Records, Our Mam's Records - 1989

Island Complex *Our Mam's Records - 2018*

SINGLES & EPS

Nevil Wanless EP (12") *Our Mam's Records - 1988*

Shrug/Archbishop Kebab (Flexi 7", Split) *Ket - 1989*

Mission From Todd (7") *Sound In Corporation - 1991*

Beardo Weirdo (7") *Rugger Bugger Discs - 1992*

The Loser/Shrug (7", Split) *Floppy Records - 1993*

Building Society (7") *Guided Missile - 1996*

Memo From Bongo Christ EP (CD-R) *1999*

Shrug In A Quango EP (CD-R) *2008*

The Bent Moustache/Shrug (7", Split)
Wormer Brothers - 2010

Too Many Cooks EP (CD-R) *2011*

Buy Shrug music at the Shrug Archive:
the-shrug-archive.bandcamp.com

Printed in Great Britain
by Amazon